T0104175

FOUR SEASONS

*A year of lost love, enduring love
and the greatest love*

.

DEE WAHL

Print ISBN: 979-8-35092-541-8
eBook ISBN: 979-8-35092-542-5

Dedication:

For Brad, my calm in the storm

TABLE OF CONTENTS

Chapter 1: All I Need Is a Miracle 1

Chapter 2: Say Goodbye.................................... 23

Chapter 3: Dancing around God 37

Chapter 4: His Life.. 41

Chapter 5: Memories...................................... 47

Chapter 6: The Autopsy and the Theories 53

Chapter 7: A Sister's Blame............................... 59

Chapter 8: Don't Forget to Say I Love You 63

Chapter 9: Moving On 65

Chapter 10: Christmas in Minnesota 71

Chapter 11: The New Year 81

Chapter 12: Grandpa Jerry 83

Chapter 13: His Grief...................................... 91

Chapter 14: The Spiral 93

Chapter 15: Saint Sadie................................... 103

Chapter 16: The Wedding 107

Chapter 17: The Drowning 111

Chapter 18: No More Second Chances 117

Chapter 19: A Broken Heart.............................. 123

Chapter 20: Dad and Shel................................ 127

Chapter 21: Dad and Me 131

Chapter 22: Choices....................................... 135

Chapter 23: Stormy Weather 139

Chapter 24: A Daughter's Blame 145

Chapter 25: Wrecked.. 151

Chapter 26: Pretending 155

Chapter 27: Going Gentle into that Good Night............. 159

Chapter 28: Grandma 163

Chapter 29: A Big Regret... 165

Chapter 30: The Letters 167

Chapter 31: Stop the Leak... 173

Chapter 32: New Suit for a Sad Girl................................ 177

Chapter 33: I Bowed on My Knees and Cried Holy........ 179

Chapter 34: Life Changes 189

Chapter 35: Horses, Motorcycles, and Yoga 191

Chapter 36: Remembrance... 197

Chapter 37: Victory Is Mine.. 199

CHAPTER 1:
ALL I NEED IS A MIRACLE

*A*s we left the hospital that morning, I asked my oldest brother, Shannon, what the date was. I wanted to burn it into my memory. It seemed very important, which I find odd now. As if I would forget a day that changed my life forever. It would be just the beginning of changes to come for our family.

I'm getting ahead of myself; let me back up a little bit. I had planned to visit my family and my boyfriend's mother. I had been with Brad for a while, but this was one of the first real visits he had with my family. I am forever grateful he entered the picture when he did. We had a couple of dinners together prior to this, but the true intimacy of his relationship with me and my family would begin now.

I arrived back in North Dakota on Thursday, October 6, 2005, and spent the night in my parents' home. My mom had just gotten out of the hospital and things had settled down again. She appeared fine, but I still accompanied her on a visit to the neurologist's office the next day.

Dr. Arazi pulled out a radiology film with a picture of Mom's brain scan. He affixed it to the backlit viewer on the wall. It came to life in front of us.

"The CT scan of your brain has some abnormalities," he said and pointed to small white spots scattered across the film. "These lesions are indicative of multiple sclerosis or MS. We will want to draw some blood and run more tests before we make a formal diagnosis."

My breath caught sharply as my stomach instantly knotted with worry. Mom took it in her stride and agreed to do the tests. We gathered our things to leave. She was not in any hurry to do the lab tests, which was odd, but I didn't argue with her.

We made a couple more stops and then I called my boyfriend, Brad, to have him meet us at Buffalo Wild Wings. Mom, Dad, my younger brother, Shel, and I had grabbed a table by the time Brad arrived. We broke bread together, and I loved every minute. I had yearned to have Brad spend time with my family. The conversation flowed, the food was tasty, and I was at a table with some of my favorite people in the world.

My nephew, Cole, had a football game that night, so Brad and I decided to go to his game. My parents elected to go home. Brad, Shel, and I jumped into Brad's Ford Ranger and headed to Steele, ND. My oldest brother, Shannon, lived there with his wife and four children. It was a forty-mile drive from Bismarck, and it was the first time Shel had been alone with us. He was unusually quiet, but we had some laughs along the way. We listened to silly songs Brad had on MP3 discs. Shel had a terrible cough, but he was recovering from a bout of pneumonia.

We met up with Shannon's family at the game. We stood with his wife, Carmen, and watched Cole play. The other kids ran around with their friends as we all tried to stay warm in the bitter cold. Brad meshed well with my family and my stomach filled with happy butterflies. However, Shel kept a watchful eye on him, which made me smile. Little brother or not, he was protective of me.

Steele won the football game and we returned to Shannon's home victorious. We sat around the oval table in the living room and traded stories and laughter. We talked about farts and other bodily functions for a good deal of the conversation. Brad adored potty humor and jumped in with his own comments. I giggled until tears came and then giggled some more.

Soon after, Brad and I left to spend the night at his mother Kathy's home. Shannon, Carmen, and Shel went to The Depot, a bar in Steele, and had a few drinks and shot pool.

Shannon later said of the evening, "It was nice to have that night with Shel. He was full of good spirits, and we were chiding each other playfully, as brothers do."

It would become a regret of mine that I did not go with them that night.

After we arrived at Kathy's, we went to bed. We awoke the next morning and spent a lazy day at home. Kathy was not quite mobile due to her recent knee surgery, so we were content to order in pizza and watch movies.

On Sunday morning, we were camped in front of the TV when I received a call from my father at 11:00 a.m.

"We took Shel to the hospital late last night. He had a terrible headache and they admitted him. They think it's meningitis. We went home to rest, but they've told us we need to come back now," he said, and his breath quavered.

"I'll get ready, Dad. Tell me when you get to the hospital and I'll meet you there," I said as I tried to sound calm. I hung up in shock. I showered and dressed as my mind raced. As I waited for my father's call, I researched meningitis on the internet. I found some disturbing information online, but that wouldn't apply to Shel. He was young and as strong as an ox. His one vice was that he was a light smoker, but that had nothing to do with this. He would be fine.

Dad called a second time. This call will stay with me for life.

"Dee, you need to come here now. It's bad," he said. His voice cracked. My father was crying.

I hung up the phone and sprang into action. Brad drove me to the hospital. I jumped out of the truck before he could slow to a stop, and I ran for the emergency room entrance. There are moments in life when seconds count and this was one of them.

I rushed up to the intensive care unit (ICU) and saw my family. Shel's room was in the corner, and I noticed the nurses wore protective gowns.

What Shel had was contagious?

A nurse approached me. My parents had told them I was in nursing school.

"I'm not in nursing school yet, but I work at Children's Hospital in Minneapolis. Please be frank with me," I said as I held her gaze.

She swallowed hard. "Shel may not make it through the night," she said. Her eyes welled up with tears.

I froze. "How is that possible?" I said with disbelief. My jaw dropped open in horror.

"We're arranging for you to view the MRI scans of his brain. The resident doctor will explain everything to you," she replied. She squeezed my shoulder before she walked away.

Moments later, Brad and I were ushered into a small room. Shel's brain scans were already tacked up on the film viewer, backlit and glaring at me.

"As you can see, there is a mass that is attacking Shel's brain . . ." the doctor began as my eyes bulged and my mind whirled.

It really didn't need explanation. I saw the culprit immediately. The human brain is divided down the middle, into two equal hemispheres. A white mass covered half of one hemisphere of Shel's brain. Swirls of white spread down toward the base of his brain and spinal cord like icy fingers. This didn't look good at all. My heart sank, even as I fought hard to hang on to my hopes for him. Brad had some medical school under his belt, and he would tell me later that he knew then. It was the worst MRI (magnetic resonance imaging, i.e., a picture of his brain) he had ever laid eyes on. He knew what I could not yet admit.

We were escorted back out to the nurses' station. A moment later, a nurse rushed up to me.

"Shel will be flown to Rochester, Minnesota and admitted to St. Mary's Hospital, which is affiliated with Mayo Clinic. Your parents want you to fly with him because of your medical knowledge," she said hurriedly, her eyes wide.

Me? What if he died and I was the only one there? What if my parents regretted that they weren't? What if I made a decision that was wrong for Shel?

"We need to know how much you weigh so they can adjust the plane accordingly," she said curtly, clipboard in hand.

"One hundred and thirty pounds," I said stonily as my fears whirred in my head.

She hurried off without a backward glance.

I was left standing next to Brad, my heart on the floor in disbelief.

I gave myself a hard shove mentally. My brain shifted in an instant and I was on the offensive, ready to do battle for Shel.

I will not fail him.

We rejoined my parents, Shannon, Carmen, and their children. We dressed in gloves and gowns to go in and say goodbye to Shel. He would be intubated for breathing and sedated for the trip. This was our last chance to talk to him. I refused to admit that it might be for the last time. Nurses cried behind their masks. Shel's eyes were closed, his bed somewhat reclined in a restful pose.

We called his name, and I willed him to answer us. His eyelids flickered.

"He squeezed my hand," Mom said. I grabbed his other hand. We continued to chime in with his name every few seconds.

"Shel, can you answer us?" the nurse called sharply. She rubbed his sternum.

"What?!" Shel exclaimed. He sounded cross and stricken. He fell silent again.

The kids took turns. They touched him and said, "I love you, Shel."

I made my voice strong. "You're going to be okay, Shel. Everything is going to be alright," I promised. I held his hand tight in mine.

We left the room so that Shel could be readied for the flight.

A nurse took me aside. She said, "You need to explain this to your parents. I don't think they understand that he might not make it through the night. He has a fifty-fifty chance. I don't think they realize the severity of the situation."

"I understand. I will explain it to them," I said softly. I watched her walk away. She didn't know that this wasn't their first time. Shel had been on the threshold of death before.

We shuffled into the family waiting room down the hall. Tears fell heedlessly now. No one was immune. I tried to hold mine in check as we sat down and faced one another.

"He might not make it through the night," I said. My throat was dry and raw. "He has a fifty-fifty chance of making it. You both need to prepare. This is serious."

Dad hung his head and gave a slight nod. Mom looked at me. Her lips quivered and her eyes were wet with tears. She said nothing in response.

Brad came back and broke the silent tension in the room. "This should be everything you need," he said as he handed me an overnight bag.

"Let's pray," Shannon said quietly. We huddled together in a circle and held hands. "Dear Lord, please be with Shel and Dee as they fly to Rochester. Please provide them comfort and strength, and help Shel fight this illness and come back to us healthy. We pray this in your heavenly name, Lord Jesus, Amen."

As I hugged everyone, a nurse seemed to appear from thin air.

"It's time to go, Dee," she said. Her hand was on my back. She led me down the hallway, where I joined the paramedics. Shel was swathed in blankets from chin to toes on a stretcher between them. Here we go.

It was a comfort to me that I knew the paramedics. I had met Annette and Dan while I worked at Medcenter One and went to an emergency medical technician (EMT) school. They would take good care of Shel on the trip. We traded greetings and I saw sad defeat in their eyes. We said little on the way to the airport. I boarded the plane. I numbly listened to the pilot's instructions as he strapped me into the seat beside him. They loaded Shel into the body of the plane and soon we were in the air.

"How is he doing?" I asked Annette. I twisted around to see her better.

She told me the medications she had given him to make him comfortable. She looked me squarely in the eye and asked, "Did you see the MRI scans?"

"Yes," I responded and I held her gaze. I saw abject sympathy and sorrow in her eyes. She looked away after a moment. The MRI was the answer to all my questions.

The sky was a crystalline blue with fluffy, white clouds. I willed Shel to wake up.

Look at this beautiful horizon! This plane ride is amazing, and you are missing it!

I reached back and touched his shoulder frequently. He was always warm.

Stay with me, Shel. C'mon, buddy. Stay with me so we can ride in a plane again and you can see the sky, too.

Green Day's song "Time of Your Life" sang in my mind like a mantra.

I hope you had the time of your life.

I silently sang it to myself. I looked out the windows. I watched the gauge the pilot had pointed out to me. He had told me how to determine the distance we were from the hospital. Two hours. One hour. Thirty minutes. I willed time to go by faster. Each minute brought help closer, and help couldn't come fast enough.

As we flew, my mind replayed the events at St. Alexius in Bismarck. They had opted against a surgery there for Shel. They were not equipped to help him if something went wrong during the operation. Our only hope was the kind of care Mayo Clinic affiliates could provide. I tried not to let my fear overtake me. Mayo was where you went when no one else could help.

What if they couldn't help, either?

I watched the clouds roll by. I prayed like I'd never prayed before.

Please, Lord. Please just let him be okay. Please, Lord, we need you.

I pictured Shel and me walking out of the hospital together, laughing over the whole ordeal. We could not lose. Wahls do not lose. Shel would be fine. We only had to make it to St. Mary's.

The flight lasted two and a half hours. I disembarked from the plane. I watched as they wheeled Shel into the hospital. The wheels touched the ground and jostled him. I heard him cough. It wasn't the kind of comfort words were, but I took it as a good sign. We walked into the hospital and into the ICU. They handed me registration papers.

They went to work on him in another room while I sat bewildered. I tried to write down the necessary information. Some of it would have to wait for my parents. My other brother, Shad, had been on a pheasant-hunting trip, and thankfully they had been able to reach him. My parents and brothers raced toward the hospital in my little car. I gave them information along their route. Unfortunately, what I had to tell them was never good.

The staff at St. Mary's did a repeat MRI. It was found that Shel's condition had worsened during the trip. The mass had spread like wildfire.

A nurse approached me and said, "We need your permission to place a shunt to drain fluid off his brain and relieve intracranial pressure (ICP)."

I nodded stonily. I signed a written consent for the procedure. Then she told me something that made me stop cold as blood drained from my face.

"Shel is doing what we call posturing, which is a sign of brain damage. One of his pupils is blown and his ICP is dangerously high. We are doing what we can to mitigate the damage." I looked at her blankly. Speechless. She put her arm around me. "Let me show you to our quiet room. You will have some privacy there and a chance to rest. We'll perform the procedure on Shel and update you as soon as we can."

I sat down heavily on a small sofa and exhaled. I hadn't even realized I was holding my breath. I was stifled by the heaviness of the room. My heart thudded painfully in my chest. I knew from working at Children's Hospital that Shel's symptoms were things that happened as a child was near death. The posturing was due to pressure on his brain. (I looked it up later and found this explanation: the Lazarus sign or Lazarus reflex is a reflex movement in brain-dead or brainstem-failure patients. It causes them to briefly raise their arms before dropping them crossed on their chests, in a position like that of Egyptian mummies.) A blown pupil meant that a pupil was dilated, also a sign of brain death. His ICP was around fifty, which should be twenty or lower. I called Shannon and explained the situation. He said they would hurry. They were still hours away.

By some miracle, I did fall asleep on that loveseat sofa. My legs dangled off the end. I knew they would come and get me if I was needed. I slept hard, dead to the world. The next thing I remember is hearing my family's voices in the hallway. I woke up immediately and opened the door. They looked at me in anticipation.

I went right to Shad and hugged him. I said, "Thank God you are here. You were here for him once and you are here for him again". There was no need to explain. He nodded and ducked away for a moment. I knew he was battling his tears.

We walked into the ICU together and stood around Shel's bed. We were all hoping for a sign from him. We touched him and told him to pull through any way that he could. I did not want to leave his side. I stood to his right bedside much of the time. I held his hand and stroked his hair.

"You have to fight, Shel," I whispered to him. "If you fight, we can walk out of here together. You have got to beat this thing, because I don't know how to be here without you."

I silently prayed. I begged and I wept. We all did. The night crept on and there was no change. We finally decided to check into a hotel across the street. We hoped for better news in the morning. Finding a hotel proved interesting. One that I had checked into via my phone was too expensive for the few hours we needed it. The next hotel was dilapidated, but the price was right, so we took it. There were two double beds and the floor. Mom and Dad took one bed, Shannon and I split the other and Shad slept on the floor. We collapsed into a few hours of precious sleep. The alarm didn't have a chance to go off. St. Mary's called early the next morning—around 6:00 a.m.—and told my parents to come over now. Shel was worse.

My parents left right away and the rest of us took turns getting ready. My thoughts nagged at me the whole time. I cut corners to get to Shel faster. My brothers hurried as well, with Shannon leaving first.

Shad turned to me. "Is he going to make it, Dee?" he asked in a strained voice. He looked me squarely in the eye.

"I don't know." I averted my gaze. But I did know. Medically, I was very scared and feared the worst. As Shel's sister, I clung to my stubborn hope and the idea that there would be a miracle.

Please, God. We need a miracle.

Shad and I crossed the street and entered the hospital. I was in a nightmare and needed to wake up. This couldn't *really* be happening. Not to Shel. I was numb and at the same time so full of emotion I didn't know what to do with it all. Embarrassingly, there were a couple of times I almost laughed out loud at the absurdity of it. I knew it was an inappropriate response. I forced myself into normalcy. We walked into Shel's room. I returned to his bedside, held his hand, and stroked his hair as before.

"Please fight, Shel. I need you. Don't leave me, please," I whispered to him with a sob stuck in my throat. I squeezed his hand. He had always listened to his big sister, and I knew he needed to listen now more than ever. I looked at him and wanted to bawl. His bottom lip was full of fluid and horribly swollen around the endotracheal tube helping him breathe. His eyes did not flicker as they did before. He did not squeeze anyone's hand. I looked at the white board on the wall. I saw the scribbled staff notes from the morning. In horror, I realized he had gone into cardiac arrest and had been resuscitated. That is why they had called Mom and Dad over. There it was, in black and white, like a kick to the head. They had given him two doses of mannitol to subdue the swelling of his brain. There was another medication listed that I did not recognize.

I pulled a nurse aside. "What happened this morning? Did he code?" I asked. I needed her to confirm it.

She nodded. "Your brother's brain almost herniated into his brain stem. His ICP was at sixty, so it was just too much pressure on his brain. I'm so sorry," she said. Her eyes were kind and soft. She gently squeezed my shoulder before moving away to tend to Shel.

I digested what this meant, and I couldn't quite come to terms with it. It didn't matter how many times I had seen it before. This wasn't someone else's family in the hospital where I worked. This was my brother, my blood, and it changed everything. I held on to hope so tight that I couldn't see anything beyond it. The miracle had to happen.

I watched the neurologist evaluate Shel. No signs were good throughout the exam.

Please, God, give us something to work with here.

I will never forget those moments in that room. I watched an evaluation similar to what I had seen several times before in my EMT and Nursing Assistant clinicals, but this time was different. My brother had no response to any of it. No response to pain, no curling of toes, no squeezing of hands. What haunts me most is the PERRLA check. Pupils are equal, round and reactive to light and accommodation. I remember the doctor opening Shel's eyelids for him and turning his head from side to side. His pupils were fully dilated, and I could see there was no response.

His eyes are like those of a dead fish.

There was no life in them. I wanted to slide down the wall onto the floor and disappear into the cracks, but I would not let myself. Even then, knowing what I knew, I did not give up on Shel. I could not let him go.

There was nowhere to go with it all. There were no answers in the quiet room. None in Shel's room. Not even in the halls, where things were more open. Dread was like a thick, wet blanket over me and the entire hospital.

"Maybe we should grab some breakfast," Shannon quietly said to the room, breaking into my thoughts.

"Yes, please go," the nurse said encouragingly. "It'll do you some good to get something in your stomachs."

"I'm not hungry," Shad said with his eyes on Shel. He moved to his bedside. "I'm staying here."

We filed out of Shel's room and read signs to find our way to the café. Even though I did not want to leave him, it was a relief to leave. To breathe new air. I walked into the café with a heavy heart. I made choices without thought. I grabbed some orange juice, a couple of strips of bacon, and some eggs. We sat down in a booth together and talked about what to do.

"We should call Aunt Vonda," Shannon said, referring to one of Dad's sisters.

"I agree," I said with a nod.

"I'm not sure that's a good idea," Dad said with a downward gaze.

"They can pray for us," Shannon persisted.

"Fine," Dad said with resignation and Shannon left the table to call her.

I did not envy Shannon for his task. So much had changed in the last twenty-four hours.

How do you explain it to someone?

The day before, Shel had raked leaves in the yard and played with Shannon's kids.

Shannon came back. "She's upset we didn't call her sooner. They would have prayed and offered us support through this," he said. He hung his head.

No one responded, and we finished our meals in silence. While I understood Aunt Vonda's feelings, I wondered wryly how that would have been possible. Everything had happened so fast, there was barely time for us to breathe, let alone tell anyone.

I ate my tasteless eggs. A song played overhead through the hospital speakers. It was called "Cruisin'," by Huey Lewis and Gwyneth Paltrow. Normally this would mean nothing to me, except that Shel had told me he liked that song. It was so odd to hear it again in the café. It was not even a new release. I wonder now if it was Shel. Maybe he used one of our last moments together to tell me it was his time.

Shad came up moments later. "The doctor has asked to meet with us," he said sadly, his face etched with worry. "That never means anything good."

We rose from the table. The remainders of our meals were thrown away. We walked stonily back to the quiet room. I sat beside my mother on the small sofa I had slept on the night before. I looked the doctor squarely in the eye. I noticed the chaplain was there, as was a registered nurse. I braced myself.

Shad was right.

The doctor took a deep breath. "We have concluded Shel's tests. I am so sorry to tell you that he is brain-dead."

My heart dropped to the floor. "Shit," my mother cursed beside me, the word ripped between clenched teeth. She grabbed my knee. The room whirled and closed in on me. The air was sucked out of the room.

I heard the doctor say various things that made sense somewhere in my mind. "He failed his apnea test, which means he is unable to breathe without the ventilator," the doctor continued. "There was no response to painful stimuli. An electroencephalogram (EEG) showed no significant activity was produced by Shel's brain. I'm very sorry that there is no chance for a meaningful recovery. There are tests we need to conduct to formally confirm our findings, but I believe the spirit that was Shel has left his body."

His words horrified me, and at the same time comforted me—I knew his pain was gone. Mom and I tightly squeezed each other's hands. Her other hand was splayed across her eyebrows, hiding her face from the rest of us.

The doctor paused and then said gently, "Do you want to be here when we remove Shel from life support?"

"When will that be?" Dad asked. He raised his head to meet the doctor's gaze.

"The tests will take a while to complete. It'll be well into the night," the doctor responded carefully.

"Is there any chance Shel could come back? Any chance at all?" Dad asked.

"I am afraid not," the doctor responded.

Dad paused awhile. "Then we will go home," he said with a defeated sigh.

My mind whirled. I wanted to stay with Shel. I didn't want to leave him there in that place, even if he was already gone from me. I imagined myself holding his hand when they turned off the machines. I wanted to be there. I wanted to say something. I looked at my father. His hazel eyes had none of their usual twinkle, and his body was slumped in a heap in a chair. He looked broken. My brothers and mother offered no argument against his request.

The heartbreak in the room was palpable. I realized it was now about the living. I decided not to make a fuss. We would go home as a family.

As everything sunk in, my emotions welled up and something in me burst. "I need to leave," I choked out as I fled the room.

I could not breathe. I ran down the hall, away from it, away from them, as sobs ripped from my throat.

SHEL!!! My darling Shel! No, no, no!!!

I shrieked at the empty hallway and grabbed a nearby wall for support. I did not know where to go. There was not a big enough room, not enough air, not enough prayer, not enough strength.

I called Brad on the phone and got his voicemail.

"Shel is dead!" I raged into the mouthpiece on a hard sob that came out of my body like a scream. "My brother is dead! How can you not answer the fucking phone! I need you! How can you not be there right now!"

I hung up the phone and fell to my knees. My body was wracked with sobs and my head was one big heartbeat. I fought to get it together. I found that I could not, but I headed back to the ICU anyway. My eyes burned and tears streamed uncontrollably. I had given up on wiping them away. I met my family in the hall and saw that I was not alone.

My mother swallowed her own pain and came to me. She put her arms around me. It shames me now, as I wanted to be the one to comfort her, but Mom got me through that day. I became her child again and she shepherded me through something I'd never experienced before. I had lost grandparents before, but this was different. Shel was my baby brother. The one I had been charged to care for when we were small. The one I had grown up with and knew the best. He was more than my brother; he was my best friend. I looked at him in that bed, knowing it was a shell of Shel. I gripped a nearby counter so hard I might have left imprints. My mother held on to me. She said comforting things and helped me as best as she could. I struggled for control. I had to say goodbye.

I touched Shel as much as possible. I stroked his hair. I felt his warmth next to me as I lay beside him on the bed. I held his hand. I breathed him in. I prayed he could hear me.

"You were the best brother I could have hoped for, Shel," I whispered to him. "I love you more than you'll ever know. You have taught me so much. I will never forget you. I will carry you in my heart for the rest of my life. I will live for you."

I tried not to think about the promise I hadn't kept. I willed myself to believe he was in a better place, which was hard. I wanted him to stay with me. Such as it was, that could never happen, so I did my best to let him go.

I cut off a lock of his hair—I loved his hair. He had thick, wavy black hair and he had been vain about it. I looked forlornly at where they had shaved his head to put in the shunt. Shel would not be pleased that they had made his hairline look so bad. The nurse put his hair in a small Ziploc bag for me.

I was desperate to take whatever I could of him home with me. The clock ticking meant something different now. My brother was beautiful, inside and out, and the physical part of him was about to be taken from me. I made handprints with his lifeless hand on sheets of paper. I had stolen the idea from Children's. It was normally done by parents who had lost children, but just as those children were precious to them, Shel was precious to me. I made enough for all of us, including my nieces and nephews.

Then I heard something that made me hand off my job to the nurse next to me. We had decided on organ donation for Shel. The representative had arrived, so we met in the quiet room once again. It helped that Shannon knew her. She was soft-spoken and kind. I was familiar with the process from working in a hospital, but I now have new respect for people who choose organ donation. It is not an easy thing to do during a very difficult time. All but Dad had agreed to do it, and so he had relented. Shel had loved people, and he would have wanted to help them.

The questions went on forever. She asked about each of Shel's body parts, with Mom giving her a yes or no answer to donation. I was brave; I wanted Shel to help as many people as possible. Then she asked about his eyes. Mom answered yes to donate and that bothered me. Shel's eyes were gentle and a beautiful blue-green hazel. They were the same color as my father's, and his father before him. If his eyes were the windows to that extraordinary soul, I wanted them to go with Shel. I did not want the possibility of bruising around his eyes at the wake, either. What I could not see I could handle, but I wanted him to look like himself as much as possible when we laid him to rest.

I interrupted her after the question was long past. "I don't want his eyes donated. I can't take that," I said and burst into fresh tears. "I'm sorry, Mom."

"It's okay, baby. I understand," Mom said and slipped her arm around me. The questions resumed and I fell silent again.

We finished and waited in the quiet room for the doctor to come and speak with us. He was kind. He expressed his condolences again and shook hands with each of us. I saw profound sadness in his eyes. I do not remember his words, only his face and expressions. He was genuinely sorry he could not do more for us.

We stopped to see Shel one last time. The nurse gave me a folder and I tucked his lock of hair and handprints inside it.

I stroked Shel's hair once again. I kissed him goodbye with my heart on my lips and whispered, "I love you, Shel. I will always love you, kiddo. I will carry you with me."

The doctor left us. We looked at each other with resolute eyes. It was time to go home.

Leaving the hospital was difficult for several reasons, the worst of which was that I was leaving without Shel. I was leaving the place where I last saw him alive. I had grown oddly attached to the starched white walls, even in as short a time as I knew them. Doubts crept into my mind. I had failed him and leaving felt like an admission of guilt.

Dad must have had the same feelings because he paused in the hallway. He went back to Shel's room. I was going to follow him, but I decided against it. I could not bear to walk into that room again. I also knew the bond between father and son is great, and Dad might want these moments alone with Shel. He needed one last touch, one last whisper, one last goodbye with his youngest child. We waited patiently for him to return and then we walked out together.

The sun was bright, almost blinding to my tired, raw eyes. I called my boss and told her what had happened. She told me to take as much time as I needed. We walked to the hospital ramp. This walk was where I asked Shannon what day it was, afraid that I would forget it. Monday, October 10, 2005, at 10:47 a.m., I left my brother at the hospital. I was so sad that no one would hold his hand that night when the life support came off. I reminded myself that it was about the living now. Shel was already gone. He wouldn't know if someone was holding his hand. I swallowed back tears. I got into the backseat of my car. Shannon was in the driver's seat, and Shad was in the passenger seat. The backseat held me, my mother, and my father. I held my mother's hand.

We decided to eat before we made the long trip home. We went to Olive Garden. It felt strange to sit in that booth after all we had been through in the past thirty-six hours.

A waitress stopped by and cheerfully introduced herself. She pulled a pad out of her apron pocket to write our orders. "Well, you're a solemn group, aren't you?" She said brightly with a smile.

Shannon's eyes met mine and we traded sad half smiles but remained silent. "We are on a long trip home," Shad said quietly. It explained everything and nothing. She smiled politely and walked away to enter our orders.

We ate and talked, and things were as normal as could be expected. It was a bit of respite from all the sadness to talk of other things and pretend that food mattered. We finished and trooped out to the car. We sat in the same order as before. I laid my head on Mom's shoulder and held her hand again. Then it hit me. The car only seated five people.

There is no room for Shel.

There had always been the six of us.

Now there are five.

Cold tears fell down my cheeks. It had happened much sooner than I had anticipated. The beginning of our family unit breaking down was supposed to begin with a parent, years from now, when they were gray-haired and in failing health. I had believed that I would lose those people I loved in an order that made sense. The loss of Shel made no sense. My stomach twisted as my own mortality hit me like a ton of bricks. Death came to us all and could come at any time.

Tears fell many times during that car ride home. My mother and I leaned on each other. I put Frank Sinatra's Greatest Hits in the CD player. He was my dad's favorite singer, and it brought a strange peace to the car. My spirit rose and fell with the music. I was relieved to concentrate on something other than what had just transpired. Sometimes it would hit me anew and a fresh wave of tears would wash over me.

Shel is brain-dead. He is not coming home.

It was a long journey home. Once the CD ended, I tried to put in Aretha Franklin's Greatest Hits, which would have been a comfort to me, but it was unanimously vetoed. The car was cloaked in silence. We stopped for food and gas periodically. We passed through Minneapolis, Alexandria, then Fargo and Valley City. I was thankful that I didn't have to make that trip home alone. Shannon and Shad took turns at the steering wheel. We made it to Jamestown when my cell phone rang. The sound cut through the silence like a knife.

It was the doctor who had cared for Shel. "I wanted to let you know that we took Shel off life support, and he has died," he said, his voice soft and sympathetic to my ear.

"Thank you for the call, Doctor. Goodbye," I said quietly, hanging up my cell. "The doctor called to say Shel just died," I announced to the car. No one responded to me. It was 10:40 p.m. Almost twelve hours to the minute from when we had left Shel that morning. I sighed with the knowledge that it was over. He was truly gone from us now.

We arrived at Shannon's home in Steele around midnight. I saw Shad's wife, Tammy, first and walked into her arms with fresh tears. We shuffled in like weary soldiers and hugged the loved ones we had left behind. Carmen's arms wrapped around me next, and then the children's. We visited for a time and then talked about going to bed. On Carm's suggestion, I swallowed some sleeping pills. My mind would not have let me sleep otherwise, even though I was exhausted. My mind raced with all that had happened. Things I couldn't change. Things that would never be the same. The gaping hole that was left in me by his absence. I crawled into bed and finally fell into a deep slumber. I did not even dream. When I woke the next morning, my eyes blearily batted open. I saw the ceiling of my brother's spare bedroom. It took a few seconds for my mind to clear. Then it hit me. My living nightmare was still in full swing. Shel was gone and I had no idea how to move forward without him.

Little brother, baby brother
Gone from me too soon
I found out I'd lost you
Just before noon
So much left undone
Sights you'll never see
A life barely begun
There's no comfort for me
Little brother, baby brother
Won't you come back to me?
I see you everywhere
Whispering from the trees
Smiling a Mona Lisa smile
Always aiming to please
How was I to know
That you'd be the first to leave?
Little brother, baby brother
I cared for you all my life
I thought we'd raise our kids together
I thought you'd find a wife
I dreamed a little dream
That turned into despair

Realizing life goes on
Even when you're not there
Little brother, baby brother
Running through the trees
Your laughter floating behind you
Like a sweet reverie
Saying without a word
You've prepared a place for me
Somewhere beyond the rainbow
Where at last we will be free

—DW

CHAPTER 2:
SAY GOODBYE

When we were kids, back on the farm, Shel and I played on a stack of haybales. We were at the top when I slipped through a hole between the bales. I was about ten at the time and had never had the wind knocked out of me before. I was on the ground looking up, unable to breathe, but I wanted so badly to breathe. I was dying. I couldn't speak. I couldn't move. Above the haystack I could see the bright, blue sky, and then Shel's little face.

He peered down at me with utter horror. "Are you okay?" he yelled.

I could not respond. I tried. I looked at him helplessly.

Finally, I squeaked out, "I'm okay. One minute."

After a few moments, I could breathe again and inhaled as if for the first time. I slowly climbed my way out of the haybales.

"That was so scary!" I told him. "I couldn't breathe!"

We climbed down and moved on to other adventures.

As I lay in bed that morning, I was back at the bottom of that haystack. Completely shattered, I wondered if I would ever be able to climb out of my despair.

I heard voices downstairs. I was groggy, as if I needed more sleep, but I decided against it. There would never be enough sleep. I could not believe Shel was gone.

I went downstairs and sat at the dining room table with Shannon. I could not think where to begin, but he knew—he was already making calls. He hung up the phone and met my gaze across the table.

"Can you call Liz and see if she can sing at the service?" he asked me, referencing our cousin and my childhood friend.

"Sure," I said with a nod.

"Can you write the obituary?" he asked, still holding my gaze evenly.

I thought for a moment. I did not relish writing the obit, but I was the natural choice. I have always enjoyed writing. As hard as it would be, I resolved to write it by the following afternoon. I needed some time. "Yes, I can," I answered him.

Brad drove from Bismarck to see me that morning, and I was never so glad to see him. I dissolved into his arms and sobbed. He held me until my tears dried and then we talked. We were supposed to be in Minneapolis closing the deal on our new house.

"I'll have to drive back tomorrow," he said gently.

Panic rose inside me, which must have been palpable, because he grabbed my hand.

"I will fly back for the wake and funeral. I will drive you home," he said.

I sighed with relief. I did not want to go to the funeral without him. I hadn't even thought of the ride home.

What happened that day I can scarcely explain, but I found myself playing in the backyard with the kids. Brad and I started a game of kickball. Shel would have loved it. He would have been right in the middle of it. I would live for moments like this over the next few months. Moments when I could laugh and see past the pain. I didn't expect it to happen on the day after losing Shel, but it did. As the children played and laughed, I knew it was the right thing to do. I played hard and cheered the kids on. Some neighborhood kids joined in, and we played until we were tired.

I could not stay with my parents. The idea of walking into the house that knew Shel so well brought immeasurable pain to me. We had a routine. I slept in the room next to his when I stayed with them. I would usually wake up first. Shel liked to stay up and watch movies till the wee hours of the morning. I would jump on his bed and tell him to get up. Sometimes he would get up right away or maybe need a few more hours. Then he would come downstairs, and we would begin our day. We would go for a bike ride or a walk or watch movies. In some ways, I reverted to childhood when I came home. We had our own language. We would play old records and dance around the house at Christmas time. We would do a pathetic version of the jitterbug and laugh at ourselves till our sides hurt. Mom and Dad would shake their heads at our silliness, but there was no stopping us. That house held so many memories that I couldn't step foot in it. I camped out at Shannon's and left my parents to grieve alone.

Brad left later that evening and we settled in for the night. The kindness of Shannon's neighbors was incredible. We were bombarded with food and cards and phone calls. The kickball game had done some good—I slept that night without the aid of pills.

I woke up the next day and my parents came to Shannon's for breakfast. It was not a pleasant visit. I found out that my father was not allowing my mother to speak Shel's name. He was belittling and berating her nonstop and I finally lost it.

"You have no right to tell my mother how to grieve. There is no excuse for talking to her in this manner. We all lost Shel, not just you," I yelled, my voice as cold as ice.

Dad did not even look at me. He got up and left. I hung my head. I should not have raised my voice at him. I do not know what it is to have lost a child. I only knew that Mom had lost her child too, and Dad was inflicting more pain on her.

I wrote the obituary later that morning. I had trouble at first, but once I got past my tears, the words began to flow. I kept it simple. I took it downstairs and let everyone read it. After a couple of tweaks, it was perfect:

Shel Wahl, 27, Tuttle, died October 10, 2005, at St. Mary's Hospital, Rochester, MN. Services will be held at 2:00 p.m. Saturday at the United Methodist Church in Tuttle with the Rev. Richard Wyatt officiating. Burial will be in the Tuttle Cemetery.

There will be no public visitation.

Shel was born November 29, 1977, in Bismarck, ND, the son of Dennis and Judi (Dougherty) Wahl.

Shel made friends easily, young and old, and genuinely loved being around people. His greatest joy was spending time with friends and family, especially his nieces and nephews. He made an indelible mark in our hearts during his short time with us and will be greatly missed.

Shel is survived by his parents, Dennis and Judi Wahl; his brothers and their families, Shannon and Carmen (Fetzer) Wahl and their children, Cole, Cody, Channa, and Chase; Shad and Tammy (Puklich) Wahl and their children, Kalene and Wyatt; his sister, Dee Wahl, and her special friend, Brad Kesselring; his grandmother, Lois Wahl; his grandfather, Jerry Dougherty; and many aunts, uncles, cousins, and friends.

He was preceded in death by his grandfather, Harold Wahl and grandmothers, Jane Kennemer and Carmen Dougherty.

My parents bowed out of planning Shel's funeral. Dad couldn't handle it and my mother chose to follow his lead. I was bewildered by their behavior. I wanted to be involved in every decision possible. I wanted to honor Shel in a way that would have pleased him. This would be the last thing that I could do for him, and I wanted it to be done just right. I know my brothers felt the same way. I sat with them and my sisters-in-law in a conference room at the funeral home. Despite our ignorance, we hammered out the details for the service.

We picked out Shel's casket together. It was one of the nicer ones, a glossy, dark-emerald green. We chose arrangements with sunflowers and a matching program. My nephew Cole wrote a lovely poem for the back of it. The obituary was posted in the paper. The wake arrived the following day.

Cole and I drove to the airport to pick up Brad.

"How was your flight?" I asked with a big hug.

He pulled back and his eyes were bright with excitement. "One of the engines died on the plane! I thought we were in trouble. People were praying out loud, thinking we were going to crash! But then they got it under control. I survived," he said with a grin.

"Are you kidding me?" I asked incredulously and smacked his arm. "It's not funny! Imagine if I had lost my brother and boyfriend in one week."

He laughed and gave me another hug. "I'm sorry! But it was amazing. I'm a little wired," he said as he threw an arm around my shoulders.

"Behave yourself," I said with a weak smile.

I shuddered at the thought of losing him. I silently sent up a prayer.

Thank you, Lord. Thank you for bringing Brad to me safely.

Cole, Brad, and I drove to the wake. I squared my shoulders and steeled myself. My family had put together two poster boards full of pictures of Shel. They were on display as I walked into the funeral home foyer. I stopped for a few minutes to admire them. I smiled one minute and cried the next. Some photos made me laugh, and then suddenly it would catch in my throat. These photos would yellow with time, while we would continue to age. Shel would remain forever young, handsome, and gone from us too soon. I bowed my head and opened the next door. Brad was right behind me.

I sobbed as soon as I could make out his features. It was impossible to prepare for such a moment. I noticed his hairline, where they had shaved him for the shunt. The lip that had been swollen now looked like a popped balloon. His eyes were closed. One of his hands rested on top of the other.

This is Shel dead.

It was the last image I would have of my beloved brother. It seemed like a joke or a nightmare. I imagined that he *was* playing a joke on me. "Ha, you've been punked!" he would say, like he was on that Ashton Kutcher show. He would throw back his head and laugh hysterically about how he had fooled me.

Show us, Shel. Jump up and show us how you fooled all of us.

He did not move. I touched his wrist, and it was over. The memory seared my brain. He was cold and wooden. I was Niagara Falls. I bent to kiss his forehead.

Goodbye, Shel. I love you so much and I always will.

I turned and found myself in Brad's arms. I cried out my sorrow into his shoulder until I was strong enough to walk away.

Family began to arrive. I saw faces I hadn't seen in a while. I hugged my aunt Arlet, or Lettie as I call her, and the tears started again.

"How are you holding up, kid?" she asked, her hazel eyes soft.

"About as well as you'd expect," I said with a tremulous smile.

"What happened?" she asked incredulously, her brows knit together in confusion.

I tried to explain. "It was so fast. We're not sure what happened, yet. There was a mass on his brain, like an infection. He was raking leaves one day and then thirty-six hours later, he was dead."

She shook her head in disbelief. "I am so sorry, Dee."

"Thank you," I said softly.

Aunt Lettie looked over at Shel thoughtfully. "I didn't know his hairline had receded so much," she mused aloud.

I smirked. "That's because it wasn't that bad. They had to shave his head to put in a shunt to drain off fluid and release pressure on his brain."

She flinched as if I had slapped her. I made a mental note to remember that my family were not medical professionals. They weren't used to hearing this kind of thing every day.

We talked a bit longer and then both moved on. I hugged aunts, uncles, cousins, and family friends. I tried to converse with everyone. I soaked in their kind words and sympathetic hugs. It was a shame that Shel could not witness their love. Although, I had a feeling he did know. I hoped it was true.

My father's mother—my last living grandmother—came to the wake. My uncle Arnold wheeled her into the room. I had spent much of my child-hood with her. We would talk for hours. She was one of those neat grandmas whom I could tell anything to, and she would always understand and love me. I could not imagine a kinder, gentler soul to have for a grandma.

I rushed over to hug her. She was nearly ninety years old. She was able to walk with a walker, but she was in a wheelchair today. I saw past the gray hair and nasal tube that supplied her oxygen when she smiled at me. No matter her age, I would always see her the way I did as a child.

"I cannot believe Shel is gone," she whispered. She shook her head with a pained expression.

"I know," I said as I held her hand. "It doesn't seem real."

Shel and I had stayed at Grandma's house countless times. We were called "the little ones." The little ones would go to Grandpa and Grandma's house while Mom and Dad were gone. I blinked back my tears. I tried to smile and changed the subject. Soon Grandma greeted other people and I moved on as well. I did run to McDonald's for her later, after she told me she was hungry. Brad and I left with three of the kids. It was nice to have that reprieve. We ate together and I laughed at the kids. I grabbed a hamburger and fries to go for Grandma.

Despite it being a wake, there were happy moments. Grandma ate her burger and fries with great delight. She was used to the bland meals at the Baptist Home where she lived, so McDonald's was a rare treat. She had an almost gleeful expression and enjoyed every bite. I hid a smile as I watched. Life goes on and joy can be found even in a McDonald's hamburger!

The kids brought light into the darkness as well. Shad's son, Wyatt, was about seven at the time. Something as serious as his uncle's wake could not dampen the young man's character. He went outside with Shannon's son Chase and had a spitting contest using the water from the cooler inside. His shoe sole was breaking apart. He would flap it loudly to amuse himself. He was terror on wheels, and I was thankful for it. Shel would have laughed so hard at all of it.

My cousin Ryan had brought his baby Juel. She was pure sunshine and her smile lit up the room. She had learned to show her "muscles" and flexed her pudgy little biceps. She scrunched up her face with the effort. It was good to laugh. Shel wouldn't have wanted all the sadness.

The funeral was the next day. I was dressed in a new pearl-gray pantsuit. I had wanted something new and honorable. I had on heels and applied makeup I knew I would cry off. I got into the car with Brad and Kathy, and we drove to Tuttle. We met at Mom and Dad's house before heading to the church.

Here we go.

We had Shel's funeral at the Methodist Church. I spent Sunday school afternoons there as a child. It wasn't the church I grew up in, but we figured the Nazarene Church would be too small, and we were right. Our family met in the back of the church. Mom was an only child, but Dad's entire family was there. They planned to walk down the aisle with us. I cherished each face and greatly appreciated that we would honor Shel as one unit.

Liz arrived and came over for a hug. I held her tight and then introduced her to Brad. "Liz, this is my boyfriend, Brad. Brad, this is my cousin Liz," I said, as they shook hands.

"It's a pleasure to meet you, Brad," Liz said with a big smile.

"It's a pleasure to meet you, too." Brad returned her smile.

"I heard you had trouble on the plane yesterday!" Liz asked with wide eyes.

"I did! Wow! It was crazy, but we made it," he responded with a laugh.

"It's so good to see you guys, but it looks like everyone's getting ready for the service. Let's chat later." Liz smiled at me and then moved on to find her seat.

I sat with Brad at our family table. The preacher stood at the front of the room and said grace with us. He had asked us if we would stand and speak about Shel. We told him that we would not be able to do that today. Cole would read the poem he had penned himself, but that would be all. As much as I wanted to, I could not conceive of speaking in front of everyone. I was hanging on by a thread. I imagine the rest of the family felt the same. It was too soon and too deep of a wound.

The pastor brought it to everyone's attention during the service that we were not going to speak. I seethed with anger from my seat. He made it sound like we were too scatterbrained to put some words together. I was disappointed in Shel's funeral. I wanted it to be cool, like Shel was, but it came off as impersonal and cold to me. It was as if I had failed him again.

The songs that Liz sang (MercyMe's "I Can Only Imagine" and Don Moen's "If You Could See Me Now") were the only saving grace in my mind. It might have stemmed from bitterness that I had to attend and admit Shel was gone, but I wanted to do more for him. Nothing seemed good enough.

I laid my favorite necklace to rest with Shel. I had worn it daily and I wanted him to have something of mine. I fumbled with the necklace as I stood in line to view him one last time. My fingers trembled so badly I couldn't unclasp it. My mother tried next and failed as well. I didn't want to break the chain and send something broken with Shel. Brad got it off for me. I had delayed others in line, but it was so important for me to give that to him.

The kids put rubber balls, marbles, and fishing lures into his coffin. I hated that they had lost their beloved uncle. Shel had wrestled and played with them as if he were their age. I looked at their tear-stained faces and unbearable sadness welled up inside me.

At the burial later, the pastor said a few words and prayed. I can't remember his words.

Shel is dead.

Throughout the service, that thought plagued me as I tried to grapple with the fact that he was gone. Afterward, those in attendance hugged us and expressed condolences. One such person was John Mehlhoff. He had gone to school with Shad and was a romantic interest of mine in my younger days. He had also befriended Shel. Shad and I were talking when he walked up to us.

He looked completely devastated. "I'm terribly sorry for the loss of Shel," he said with tears in his eyes.

"Thank you, John," I said, which was seconded by Shad.

"I truly wish I had spent more time with him," he said longingly, his eyes kind and soft as they met mine.

I knew what he meant without saying it. "It's okay, John. I truly believe he's in a better place now," I reassured him.

"Yeah, John, don't worry. It's alright," Shad said. He clapped him on the shoulder and shook his hand.

"Will we see you at the reception, John?" I asked.

"No, I can't come. We have a new baby at home that's sick, so I don't want to stay away too long, but I had to pay my respects," he said sadly.

"Well, I'm glad you did," I said gratefully.

John's gaze met mine. "You'll have to invite me to your wedding," he said softly.

I gave him a puzzled look, and he answered with a smile.

"I hope the baby gets well soon. It was so good to see you. We'll miss you at the reception," I said with a warm hug.

Shad hugged him as well. And then he was gone.

I pondered John's sorrow and guilt for a moment. John's a Christian and I believe he feared that he had failed to bring Shel to Christ. Before that moment with John, I hadn't thought about regrets other people might have regarding Shel. Instinctively, at that moment, I believed what I had told John. Shel had to be in a better place. If I didn't believe that I would have been on my knees. It was the only thing that gave me strength.

We headed back to have a reception at the church. There were so many people I was happy to see there. I hadn't learned the art of gracefully floating around the room, but I tried to talk to everyone. A few that stand out in my mind are Pastor Bob and Maggie Annon, whom I had met at the tender age of fifteen. I still consider him my pastor, and Maggie had always been a close friend. They were in their early sixties, but they were ageless to me and an incredible comfort.

A former classmate of mine named Tina was also there, but to my own chagrin, I found she hadn't changed much. As children, we had been joined at the hip. As adults, our "opposites attract" connection didn't hold much water anymore. We didn't have much in common and she had hurt me one too many times.

She ran over and gave me a fierce hug. She cried on my shoulder. "We must stop this now. Whatever we were fighting about doesn't matter. I miss my best friend."

I hugged her back and mumbled in agreement. I was too numb to return her emotion. It was a bad time to make the appeal. I didn't have anything to give to her and I knew it. We played half-hearted phone tag for a month after his funeral. The phones silenced when we were never able to make contact. Truth be told, I didn't try very hard.

Several people from our hometown church were at the reception. They knew me better as a young girl in pigtails. I was "Dee Dee" to them, and their voices were like a balm to my ears. It was a comfort to know they would be as familiar to Shel as they were to me. I entertained the idea that Shel could see them through my eyes.

We had coffee and ate bars and cookies and reminisced. I figured it would be horrible, that I would cry the whole time. It wasn't like that at all. It was a comfort to talk to each person. Time flew by. Before I knew it, the room full of people had dwindled to a few stragglers.

We divided up flowers and plants that had been given to the family in honor of Shel's passing. I made sure to grab the gift from Kathy. It was a beautiful philodendron, leaves lush and green, a bright red bow fastened to it. It immediately became the "Shel plant" to me. I would take good care of it. For once, I would have a plant that I would not kill. I named her Melody. I figured if I made it personal, I would remember to water her.

We said our last goodbyes and then it was just the family, gathered around our cars, to hug one last time. I found myself in my father's arms. Dad was a recovering alcoholic and I feared Shel's death would throw him into a relapse. I worried that if it did, he would not be able to conquer it this time. I stood with him, apart from the others.

"Dad, if you ever feel weak, just call me. Doesn't matter what time of day," I told him. "Any time you need someone to talk to, I am there."

He nodded and wiped away a tear. "Thank you."

"I mean it, Dad. Don't give in. Be strong. Shel would want that," I said gently. "Hold on, and when you can't, hold on to me, the boys, and Mom. Call any of us."

He hugged me again, harder this time. He pulled back and met my gaze with tears in his eyes. "I have really good kids," he said with a tremulous smile.

I smiled back at him, squeezed his hand, and then climbed into the car with Brad and Kathy.

I was exhausted by the time we got back to Kathy's. I don't remember much of that night. I carry only one memory that I can recall. I went to the bathroom and then downstairs to change into comfier clothes.

The dam that had held back my emotion from the day broke and I let out a scream that didn't sound human. Brad caught me up in his arms. My heart splintered in my chest. I screamed and cried till my throat ached. I clung to him and let the sobs wreck me. My grief washed over me. I was engulfed and spit out again. Brad stood strong and weathered the storm until I was able to come up for air.

CHAPTER 3:
DANCING AROUND GOD

I consider myself a spiritual person, but I don't cleave to a specific religion. I was raised as a Nazarene (their beliefs are like that of Baptists), but my parents weren't strict about it. If we wanted to go to church, we could go, but it wasn't something I was made to do.

Dad was raised in a devoutly Nazarene household. He was made to go to church every Sunday, no excuses. As a result, when he became an adult, he had little use for church or religion. Dad believed in God; he prayed. He just didn't embrace it like his parents or siblings. He fancied himself as the "black sheep" of the family. He set a Christian foundation that he was fine with his parents cultivating within us, but his children would not be made to go to church.

Sometimes Mom or Grandpa and Grandma would take us to church, but not Dad. I can only remember a couple of special occasions that he attended. There was one year that I had lines during a Christmas play, and I was so proud to know he was in the audience. We also were not baptized as babies. He wanted it to be our choice.

I had spent most of my life with God on the back burner. I started my relationship with Him when I was about eight years old. Dad was drunk and being mean to me. I walked to the mailbox at the end of our driveway and asked the Lord to come into my heart and take care of me. As my tears fell, it seemed right to open my heart up to Him as Grandma had taught me to do. I felt better afterward, my burden lighter.

As I grew, I turned to Him when I felt hurt, scared, or unhappy. When times of strife came, I knew to go to Him. The rest of the time, I kept Him waiting in the wings. I preferred to dance alone on the stage of life. I brought Him in as a side show when things got a little rough.

As a teenager, I was shy socially. I liked to stay at home with Mom and Dad most of the time. Sometimes I went out with Tina or Carmen, but I lived a sheltered life for the most part. I had been taught to be a good girl and unlike most teenagers, I didn't rebel much. I was that rare kid that wanted to please my parents.

I liked to go to church functions geared toward teens—the occasional lock-in (I would be locked in for a night at the YMCA with my friends from church), a night of bowling, pizza at someone's house, etc. My favorite was Teen Camp, which was held once a year. It was held in South Dakota. My grandparents got Dad's permission and then arranged it for me. I always went with Aunt Lettie and Liz. It was a nice way to socialize with other young Christians, learn about God, play sports, and go to the big dance at the end. It was one week out of the year when it was okay for me to openly love God. I would pray on my knees at the altar. I would sing for all to hear. I was self-conscious about doing this back home, but at camp I reveled in the Lord. I loved that feeling that would remain for a few weeks afterward. I would have an inner peace and happiness that had me walking on air. I would pray a lot at first, talk to Liz more (she was steady and strong, firm in her faith, unlike me), and read my Bible. And then, as the weeks fell away, I would slowly go back to placing the Lord on the back burner.

As an adult, I became wilder, living out my teen years in my twenties. I drank, did the club scene for a while, and had a couple of serious boyfriends. It was a real roller coaster at times. My innocence gave way under some hard knocks that life dealt me. I disappointed my family and myself at times, but it was the normal stuff that happens as you grow up. I dated the wrong guys, lived above my means at times, and was in and out of college. I was earnestly trying to figure out what I wanted to be when I grew up. I knew God was there and I leaned on Him occasionally, but I had both feet firmly planted in the secular world, and it didn't occur to me to mind.

And then I met Brad, who would become the love of my life. At this point in time, the fact that he was not spiritual or religious registered as a potential issue on my radar, but it was not a deal breaker. In fact, at times, his scientific and fact-based views made sense to me. I had danced with and around God all my life, but now I was letting Him sit out of more and more dances. I never turned my back on Him—I couldn't bring myself to do that—but I began to see things differently. I was exploring other beliefs and points of view.

When Shel wound up in the hospital and I sent up that little prayer from Kathy's, it was the first I had prayed in a while. I brought God out of the wings and back on stage with me. And once He was there, it did not occur to me to let Him go again. Maybe I would never be Mother Teresa, but I was better with Him than I ever was without Him.

CHAPTER 4:
HIS LIFE

*S*hel Harold Lyn Wahl was born on November 29, 1977, to Dennis and Judi Wahl. He was the youngest of four children. My mother said that he was her "surprise" baby. My parents thought they were done having kids, and then Shel came along.

He was the biggest baby she delivered, at just over 8 lb. He became my buddy from the very beginning. We were only two and a half years apart. Shannon and Shad were also a little over two years apart, with four years between Shad and me. As it was, they paired off and Shel and I did. Not to say that there weren't times we all played together, especially in our younger years. We used to play *Star Wars*. Shannon would be Luke Skywalker, Shad was Han Solo, I was Princess Leia (of course), and Shel, laughingly, was Chewbacca. We used the sickles from the swather, or various other machinery parts, as our laser guns. Dad's boat was our *Millennium Falcon*. We would play on stacks of haybales and pretend the ground was lava, with two of us trying to push off the other two. There was also football. Shannon and Shel were a team, leaving Shad and me to pair off. Shad gave us football names; I was "Noodle," since I was so skinny, and Shel was "Meat" because he was a well-rounded little guy. We were as thick as thieves back then.

I'm not going to lie and say we had the greatest childhood. In some ways it was. As a kid, the farm was fun. There was so much to explore, and I was happy to play in an endless backyard. We would use our own wits and what was at hand to entertain ourselves.

We would weave in and out of the lush trees that lined our property with agile footsteps. Shel was my partner in these endeavors. Shannon and Shad grew older and had to help Dad farm. Shel and I were younger and babied more. I was the little sister to the other two, but with Shel, I was the big sis, and I wielded my power with great relish. Somewhere along the way, I had browbeaten the poor kid enough that he knew to let me have my way. It's also possible that what we did together didn't matter much to him. Shel was content to play and spend time with me. He was easygoing and kind-hearted. He had a "Mona Lisa smile" in pictures—none of his teeth showed. His mouth would turn up at the corners, his expression pleasant and affable.

As I mentioned before, Dad was an alcoholic. This is where the not-so-good part of our childhood comes into play. I used to think my dad would be the best father in the world if he didn't drink. It made him mean. Every three days or so, he would binge-drink and put us through hell. We were fearful as children. We walked on eggshells and tried not to set off his temper. The older boys had it worse than Shel and me, especially Shannon. Maybe it was because I was the only girl and Shel was the baby, but for whatever reason, the older boys took more flak from him. I can remember fistfights at Christmas between Dad and the older boys. There were countless harsh words and arguments. It was a challenging life at times.

Things happened along the way that made it still harder. One day, Shel had an accident when he was seven years old, which changed his life and altered our family dynamics forever. I was home, sick with pneumonia, and Shannon was home due to leg muscle pain. Only Shad and Shel rode the bus home from school that day. The bus driver stopped at the end of our driveway and Shad got off the bus. He turned around in time to see Shel get struck by a grain truck. The bus driver (who was not our usual driver but his wife) failed to turn on the hazard lights that signal to the driver of the vehicle behind that children are disembarking. Shel was hit and pushed by the truck for several yards before the teenaged driver, Jeremy, realized what had happened.

Shad ran down and waved his arms frantically, screaming at Jeremy to back up. Shel was lying injured on the road while Shad ran to the house. He told my parents what had happened, and my father ran as fast as he could to Shel's side. Dad hadn't bothered with his shoes. He ran down the long, graveled driveway barefoot, fearing the worst.

I was taking a nap when all of this was happening. Suddenly, I woke to the sound of chaos. Blurry-eyed and confused, I came downstairs and saw Shel sprawled on the kitchen counter. He screamed and cried words I couldn't understand. Handkerchiefs and towels covered his leg, and they were soaked through with his blood.

The ambulance from a neighboring town had been called. In the meantime, the first responders from Tuttle were there to assist. They applied pressure to Shel's wounds and tried to keep him calm. My grandparents were there too, and Grandma ushered me into the living room. I didn't get to see much. I only knew that Shel was hurt bad. I began to cry. Grandma told me that Shel was run over by a grain truck. Before I could wrap my ten-year-old mind around what that meant, Shel had been loaded into the ambulance and was gone.

Shel didn't come home for a long time. Shannon, Shad, and I lived with Grandma and Grandpa during this time, while Mom and Dad spent every moment possible with Shel at the hospital. It was first thought that he might not live through his injuries. He was feverish and septic. When he made it over that hurdle, the doctors then thought his leg would not be saved. Shel had nasty abrasions on his forehead, lacerations on his left hand, and his left leg had been split open to the bone from his hip to his ankle. There were several surgeries performed to try to save his leg. The doctors would think they had been successful, but then more gravel would be found in Shel's wound, which meant another surgery and then another.

I missed Shel terribly; I longed for him to come home. I didn't get to visit him very often, and there were so many things I didn't understand. I knew he had a big cast on his leg and that he was too injured to leave the hospital. Shel missed a ton of school. He had stuffed animals that accompanied him into every surgery. His favorite was his Sad Sam puppy. One such toy became mine. As sick as Shel was, he told Mom and Dad to bring home a Meddy bear for me (the hospital issued these bears to children having surgery). It became my favorite bear. A sad substitute for my little brother's company, but I treasured it.

After nearly two months in the hospital, Shel came home. His leg was saved, but he was on crutches. The cast became smaller and smaller over time, and then one day it was gone. However, Shel would always have a scar the length of his leg. But he was whole and still my brother and playmate. I didn't know about the nightmares that would plague Shel for years. He confided in Mom about them. He would watch TV and suddenly be scared that a truck would crash into the house and get him.

There was a trial that followed. My parents settled out of court with the family of the teenager that had driven the grain truck. Jeremy happened to be the older brother of my best friend, Tina. Our parents remained friendly despite the ordeal, but others would not be as gracious toward my family.

My parents had decided to sue the Tuttle school district and the bus driver. The bus driver's wife was not licensed to drive a school bus. Therefore, the school and the bus driver were liable for Shel's accident. Some people in Tuttle understood, and some loathed us for filing the lawsuit.

Long story short, we won the trial. Shel was awarded a monetary settlement as a result. At the age of eighteen, Shel would start receiving a lump sum every five years. My parents' dogged determination paid off. I know they never regretted the fight they'd endured, despite the sour taste it left with the townspeople afterward.

Shel was coddled even more by my parents after the accident. I can understand why; a traumatic event like that changes a person. Shel grew up and graduated while living with Mom and Dad. He claimed the rooms upstairs as his own. But one day, he got into some trouble with the law. He drove while under the influence of alcohol. He got caught driving without his license. I heard stories from other family members about Shel's antics and it made me sad. I hoped he wasn't heading down the same path as our father.

Shel did figure things out with time. Whether it was common sense or that he was without a license and unable to get into a jam, I'm not sure. He started to behave himself when the next life obstacle came along.

It was found that Shel had deep vein thrombosis (DVT) in his leg. He had also suffered some seizures. He went on medication for his blood disorder and seizures. The doctor cautioned my parents against leaving him alone for too long.

The brush with the law and the seizures kept him from getting his license back. It was social death for him in Tuttle. The one time he tried to drive, he was reported by one of the townspeople. Hence the "driving under suspension" debacle.

Shel was in his mid-twenties and tied to home much of the time. He had to depend on Mom and Dad a great deal, and I knew it bothered him. He tried to make the best of it and rarely complained. He worked out in a makeshift gym in the basement and would go for long walks. He ran a bar that Dad owned. He tried to keep himself busy.

Eventually, though, Dad lost the bar. The town board voted to revoke his liquor license when it was reported that Shel had served minors. Dad fought hard, but he didn't have too many friends in that town. He was indignant about it, but the rest of us were relieved. Dad had quit drinking, and we hoped this would be his last bout with alcohol. The bar was too much temptation for him, and the liquor license revocation felt like a blessing.

Dad was on his second attempt to quit drinking. He had already been to West Central Human Service Center, where he was committed for thirty days and received counseling for his addiction. That was attempt number one. He had nearly died. He had another brush with death two years later when he began drinking again. And unlike the first time, he remembered this experience. He had problems with his short-term memory and knew that some damage had been done. He finally believed his doctors and his family when we told him he would die if he continued to drink. He eventually got sober.

Mom told me that Shel was disappointed in Dad's behavior after he stopped drinking. He thought he would end up with a new father. Dad's domineering personality remained even when he was sober; it just wasn't as volatile. Shel was glad Dad had quit but mentioned to Mom that he had hoped there would be more change in Dad.

I don't think Shel liked Dad too much. I wouldn't want to speak for him, but I knew his heart well enough to say that Dad disappointed him. Shel didn't like how hard Dad came down on him about things. He abhorred the way Dad would berate and belittle Mom all the time. Shel's tenderhearted nature conflicted with Dad's brash way of handling things. They loved each other, but there was always some discord there. They couldn't quite relate to each other.

CHAPTER 5:
MEMORIES

*S*hel was a fun, wonderful person. I know everyone says that when they lose someone they love. Sometimes I'm sure it's true, but at other times, people feel obligated to say such things in respect. I have often thought that not everyone can be as great as they are portrayed in death. There are mean, horrible people out there, but somehow everyone becomes a hero when they die. People like to keep up appearances. In this case, Shel deserves the credit.

Shel had the heart of a lion and was a true friend. He knew my faults as well as I did, but he loved me *for* them, not *despite* them. Shel had an incredible knack for loving all of a person. He had a way of seeing all of you. There is no way I can convey everything he was, but the following are a handful of my memories of him.

One of the last times I was with Shel, we drove out to Josephine Lake. The lake is close to my parents' home; many of our childhood memories were made there. We were going to go for a swim. It was July, blisteringly hot, and it sounded like a good idea to take a dip, until I saw the murky depths of the water. I was going out later, so I decided to skip the swim. I sat on the dock and soaked my feet instead. Shel took one look, considered my thoughts on the matter (because he was going out with me), and took a swan dive into the lake. It's maybe not worth mentioning, but it spoke of his character to me. I was being a total girl, worried about my hair, not having time to shower, etc., but he didn't care. He dove into that water like it was an old friend, with no thought given to how dirty and algae-ridden it looked. It was what he wanted to do at that moment, and he did it. No excuses.

Christmas was special for Shel and me. We became kids again and danced around the house. We would play old Christmas records, trim the tree, and drive Mom and Dad nuts with our antics. Movies like *The Christmas Story*, *It's a Wonderful Life*, and *How the Grinch Stole Christmas* were played nonstop. We built snowmen and went sledding with our nieces and nephews. We were twenty-somethings going on eight years old. Shel loved Christmas as much as I did. He relished the traditions we had and threw his heart into it every year. If I couldn't make it back for it, I was always saddened that I wouldn't see him. It was like going through the holidays without my right arm. There was nothing too silly, no movie we'd seen too many times, no game that was too lame to play. Shel loved it all and I loved him for it.

I brought a kite home to Mom and Dad's one weekend. Once again, we were in our twenties but still kids at heart. It was a big, jauntily colored kite and we couldn't wait to get it up in the air. We went over to the school's lawn, which was right by my parents' home, and tried our best to fly the kite.

I laughed till tears came as Shel ran back and forth across the lawn.

"Come on, baby, fly for Daddy!" he yelled. He tripped while running and turned a somersault in the grass.

He came up with a grin and tried again. It was windy, but not quite windy enough. We had the best time being complete dorks, trying to fly a kite on a day that just wouldn't cooperate with us.

I was back at home on another weekend, and it poured rain the entire time. I stood at the bay window facing the street and noticed something running across the road.

"What is that?" I asked Shel in complete bewilderment.

He joined me at the window. "I'm not sure," he said.

"I'm bored. Let's try and catch it," I said with a laugh.

"Okay," Shel said without question.

We put on our coats and headed outside. I readied my parents' garbage can. I watched my brother, his hair plastered to his forehead, herd this thing in the pelting rain. He chased it up the driveway and into the garbage can. It was a muskrat! We laughed until our sides hurt and held the muskrat captive until our parents got home. We went to show them our prisoner, but the joke was on us—he chewed his way through the garbage can. This made us laugh hysterically, while our mother yelled at us.

When we were little ones (I was about eight, so Shel was around six years old), Dad was drunk and decided to have it out with our mother.

"Get the hell out of this house! Go outside and play," he yelled at us. His voice and eyes burned through me and Shel.

We did not say a word in response. Shel and I hurriedly put on our snowsuits. I knew Dad wanted to say nasty things to our mother, and he didn't want us to overhear him. We bundled up, but it was freezing outside, and soon it was too cold for us to be out. We were too scared to go back in the house. Shel and I sought refuge in an old broken-down car in our garage. We still shivered, but at least we were out of the wind. I held onto Shel for warmth as much as comfort.

There were times as a child that I endured something horrible, but I was unable to do anything about it, and this was one of those times. While we waited inside that broken-down car, I started to sing softly to Shel. Church hymns, lullabies, anything I could think of to sing.

"Do you like my voice?" I asked him shyly.

"Yes," he said forlornly, his voice trembling. "It makes me feel better when you sing."

I sang to him for a long time, until my voice turned raspy. I wanted to cry, but I didn't. I held Shel in my arms, and I wanted to protect him. We sat like that for what seemed like an eternity, and then Mom was there. She walked us back to the house.

Dad had finished his rant and had retired to the sofa to pass out. As children, we learned to like it when he "napped." It meant a reprieve from his drinking and foul temperament. We would be quiet so that we wouldn't wake him. We understood at a young age that he needed time to sleep, or he would wake up and still be horrible to us. Shel and I were a comfort to each other through years of Dad's abuse. I don't know how I would have gotten through it without him. We were each other's rock.

Shel was an excellent chess player. He had a knack for knowing which moves to make and even beat his older brothers at it. Shel also loved playing video games. His favorites were *Streets of Rage* and *Mortal Kombat*. I would come back for the weekend and play with him for as long as I could stand it (he could play for hours!). His skills far exceeded mine, so we usually played as a team against the machine. Shel knew all the button combinations and the "tricks" of the characters. He tried to teach me, but I was a lost cause. I would practice my kicks and moves at the side of the screen, away from the bad guys.

He fought the machine like a champ and then yelled, "Will you quit practicing and help me? I'm getting my butt kicked over here!"

I did a few more "practice" round house kicks for good measure. "Keep your pants on," I said with a laugh.

Finally, I'd help him beat the monster at the climax of the game's level. It became this joke between us that I'd let him fight off all the bad guys while I practiced to the side. I always helped him at the end, before he was completely pulverized.

Shel and I had fun unloading the car after shopping trips to Bismarck. This was not a fun task by default, but we made a game out of it. Mom would buy an exorbitant amount of food and supplies, since she had four kids and didn't get to Bismarck too often. We learned to have fun with it by tossing things to each other. Especially toilet paper.

"Go long!" I said, throwing the economy-sized toilet paper package at him.

He caught it with ease. "Touchdown!" he yelled, spiking the toilet paper.

"And the crowd goes wild!" I shouted.

We both cupped our hands around our mouths to simulate a crowd cheering.

This continued into our adult years, after Mom and Dad had moved into our grandparents' house in Tuttle. We knew how it looked to the neighbors but couldn't care less. It usually egged us on if we noticed someone watching us.

Shel was a little vain. I found this endearing about him. A little narcissism never hurt anyone if you can back it up, and Shel *was* handsome. He had thick, wavy dark hair and big hazel eyes that were a lovely shade of blue flecked with green. He had an easy smile, and he didn't so much walk as he did stroll.

Shel's looks and natural charisma, coupled with just-below-the-surface vulnerability, intrigued the ladies. He told Mom once that he didn't have to do or say anything; he would walk into a room and the girls would come to him. He liked to needle me about it.

"I am so good-looking! Damn, how did I get so good-looking?" he would ask incredulously, standing in front of the mirror like The Fonz.

"Man, it's getting deep in here. Where are my boots?" I said to his reflection, rolling my eyes.

"I am sooo beautifullll to meeeee! Can't you seeeee?" he sang, Joe Cocker style, just to rile me. He ran his fingers through his hair and tossed his head like a supermodel.

Inevitably, I would burst into laughter. "Seriously, how did I end up with you as a brother? Oh, the vanity!"

He became my partner in crime and silliness at a young age. Our poor mother tried to keep a handle on us, but we were mischievous and naughty to the core. We would taunt her as she was trying to cook and then run away when she chased us with the flyswatter. It was a game we never tired of playing. Shel and I stole cookie dough and food she was prepping for dinner behind her back. We jeered and made faces at each other and Mom. She told us that our faces would stay that way, but we knew better.

Mom told me that Shel was not a picky toddler when it came to food. He would eat whatever she put in front of him during school months. The minute I was home for the summer and said I didn't like something, he stopped liking it.

I didn't realize it until later, but Shel worshipped his big sister. He listened to me, patterned himself after me, and unconditionally loved me. I ate it up, because I was the little, insignificant sister with my two older brothers. Shel adored me, and I haven't found that kind of love often enough in life. I will always miss his devoted love, because the older I get, the more I realize it is a treasure to have that in your life.

CHAPTER 6:
THE AUTOPSY AND THE THEORIES

*S*hel was not like the rest of us. He didn't crawl as a baby; he scooted on his butt. He walked and talked later than we did. He potty-trained at an older age, and he wet the bed occasionally as a child. Shel also had difficulty with certain words (for instance, as a teen he would pronounce breakfast as "breakficks").

Shannon, Shad, and I had all been good students. Shel was held back in second grade due to his accident and, thankfully, it was the only grade in which that happened. He really struggled with school and usually came home with Cs, Ds, and Fs, much to the chagrin of our father. Dad prided himself on his intelligence, so it pained him that his youngest child didn't quite make the grade. My parents never got him checked out for these things. Maybe it was assumed that he was "slower" than the rest of us, or maybe it was because we were poor.

Shel was, however, quite smart about certain things. He loved and excelled at strategy games and puzzles. He liked to draw. He made up characters and sketched them. I came to think of Shel as artistic, unique, and very much his own person. Not less than we were, just *different*. We all had plans to leave and go to college or work after graduation, but Shel never talked about dreams like that. He lived with Mom and Dad and took his time with things.

Eventually, he found his wings and wanted to leave the nest and start his life. He began to work toward that, but then he had his health issues and brushes with the law. It delayed his freedom. Ultimately, it would be a freedom he would never know.

We found out something about Shel in the hours before his death that I wish we had known earlier, because it explained many things about him. St. Alexius did some CT scans after Shel was admitted for his illness. It was his first time at St. Alexius, since my parents had just switched hospitals.

The doctor asked Shannon and my parents some questions, and it was like he had known Shel all his life. He described the poor grades, delays in motor milestones (walking, talking, toilet training), difficulty with problem-solving, and his seizures. Shannon asked how he knew all this information about Shel. The doctor replied that the CT scan showed that Shel had a rare birth defect called agenesis of the corpus callosum (ACC). He was surprised that we had no idea he had it. (I can only speculate as to why Medcenter never told my parents, as he had CTs done there, as well.) The doctor explained that ACC is a rare congenital disorder, in which the band of tissue connecting the two hemispheres of the brain fails to partially or completely form.

In Shel's case, it had not formed at all. The severity of the disorder depends on the individual. It happens in the womb, between the fifth and sixteenth week of pregnancy. In most cases, the cause of the disorder is unknown. Research suggests that some possible causes may be chromosome errors, inherited genetic factors, prenatal infections or injuries, prenatal toxic exposures, structural blockage by cysts or other brain abnormalities, and metabolic disorders. Some people affected by ACC live normal lives, while others suffer from physical abnormalities, autism, or mental retardation. We realized Shel had been lucky.

I was unbearably saddened by the news. After some research, I learned that ACC sufferers have a low perception of pain. I couldn't help but wonder if that might have contributed to Shel's death. Perhaps his defect had aided in his demise because he hadn't realized he'd been in pain right away. This would've given the mass in his brain more time to grow before he realized something was wrong.

If Shel had been diagnosed in his early years, it would have made the person that he was easier to understand. It would have alleviated some heartache for my family. I learned to accept Shel as he was, and I was glad of that, but there were times I teased him about things. It added a dose of guilt to the top of my mountain of grief.

Worst of all, Shel was deprived of peace of mind. Nothing that happened to him had been his fault. If our family had known Shel had the disorder, it would have made all the difference in the world. We could have helped him. As it was, he died before we could tell him that he had ACC.

When he died, the hospital asked us if we wanted an autopsy. Dad had worked in a mortuary as a young man, and the thought of putting his son through that was more than he could bear. Somehow, we talked Dad into an autopsy of Shel's brain. When I got the results, it was not enough information. I asked one of the Pediatric Intensive Care Unit (PICU) doctors at Children's, and he confirmed my fears.

"This states that he had an infection," Dr. Maslonka said gently as his eyes met mine.

"It doesn't say what caused it?" I asked hopefully.

"No. It was a big infection—a mass across much of his brain—but there's no evidence as to what caused it, according to this report. I'm sorry."

I wanted to scream in frustration. My medical mind needed to know why it happened. I was angry at Dad's weakness. I yelled at him from all corners of my brain without saying a word, from five hundred miles away.

How could you not want to know what happened? How could you deprive me of finding that out? He can't feel the autopsy; he is dead! Don't you understand? Life is for the living, and I want to know why he left us!

The need to know didn't wane. There were times that I wanted his body exhumed. Shel's body could tell us the secrets that I wanted to know. I would have ordered the exhumation if it were up to me, but my family wouldn't have allowed it. It wouldn't bring him back, but that desire to know the answers made me want to scratch out my own eyes.

I was left with theories about what had happened.

Had everything started with his pneumonia?

Did a blood-borne bacterium find its way to his brain?

Dad had owned an old bar and hotel that he wanted to renovate. He had Shel handle most of the demolition work for both buildings.

Did he inhale something? Asbestos or something worse?

Mom and Dad also had pneumonia. I suspected everything was linked together.

Was there mold in the ductwork at their house?

Had they all had the same infection?

Why did they live when Shel died from it?

I drove myself crazy with all my questions. I turned into Nancy Drew and spent hours on internet research. I would never know the truth, but I came up with a theory that allowed me to sleep at night. I believe that Shel contracted pneumonia from his demolition work. He inhaled some airborne pathogen that went to work on his body. He passed that infection on to Mom and Dad, but they were able to recover from it. For Shel, it went from his lungs into his bloodstream. Once in his bloodstream, it traveled to his brain and set up shop. It grew inside his brain until it finally became enough of a nuisance that Shel noticed it. But by the time he noticed it and got that splitting headache, it was too late. It was a juggernaut that would not be stopped, and it claimed his life.

If my theory was right, there was nothing any of us could have done. It assuaged my guilt at not being able to save him. I made him the promise that he would be okay because it was all I could do, and I wanted to believe it. I said something to give him hope, and when someone is in a fight for their life, that's the right thing to do.

CHAPTER 7:
A SISTER'S BLAME

I was angry about so many things after Shel died. I don't even know where to begin. I was mad at schoolmates and friends that didn't appreciate him enough. My resentment screamed at me from the depths of my mind:

Why is so-and-so still alive? Why does he get to live?

He isn't half the man Shel was, and it's not fair that he gets to live and Shel doesn't!

I would kick him in the balls if I ever saw him again for treating Shel like he did!

This anger subsided over time, but there are still people that I'd like to meet in a boxing ring. There was a so-called friend of Shel's that had locked him out of his truck when they got into trouble with some boys from a neighboring town. He locked Shel out to save his own skin and Shel was badly beat up, with no one to help him.

Another "friend" took advantage of Shel when he was bartending for Dad. He turned the bar into his personal playground and goaded Shel into pouring several "prairie fire" shots (whiskey and hot sauce). Once Shel obliged, he refused to pay and told Shel he had to drink them all. To avoid wasting liquor and to appease his friend (because Shel wanted to be liked), he drank them all. Those shots are awful, and I seethed with anger knowing what Shel had been through that night. I hated how he was used and abused by people. I likened it to someone kicking a puppy. Shel was too kind and decent for the treatment he received on many occasions in his life. Some of that is part of life—everyone struggles and is mistreated at times—but it added to my grief. The things that could never be made right bothered me more than anything else.

I was angry with my parents for not having medical insurance for Shel. I had worked in hospitals long enough to know how things worked. I knew he was treated like a second-class citizen. Maybe a test wasn't done because there was no insurance. Maybe a diagnosis wasn't revealed because my parents couldn't pay for treatment. My mind categorized and filed all the possibilities that meant that Shel had received second-rate care.

Why in God's name wasn't that kid on insurance!?

That's an excellent question. The simple answer is that my father was a farmer, and it just didn't figure into "finances." It's a hard concept to grasp, especially for those that are employed by a company that provides them with medical insurance. However, when a person is self-employed as a farmer with four kids, it's not always so simple. Mom and Dad paid for everything out of pocket when it was needed. When one of us broke a leg or had pneumonia, they took us to a doctor. There were no yearly preventative checkups at my house. Something had to be wrong that couldn't be fixed. At times, I'm sure the amount was more than they could pay, and it became a hospital write-off. My parents did the best they could with what they had. They fed us, clothed us, and took care of us with limited finances.

I tried not to pass judgment on my parents, but I saw the lack of insurance as a contributor to Shel's death. Hospital workers look down on people without insurance. I couldn't rule it out as a possibility; I entertained the idea that he might still be alive if insurance hadn't been an issue.

I was also angry at Shel.

I had to forgive him for his part in his own demise. He hadn't fully recovered from his pneumonia. *Why had he raked leaves in the yard with the kids? Did he ignore his pain, so he wasn't a bother to our folks? Did he have headaches before and didn't tell anyone? Why didn't he fight harder? Why didn't he call me? Why did I have to lose him so soon? Wasn't there anything more he could have done to save himself?*

Maybe I could have saved him if I had known the full picture.

Why couldn't he just live?

I lost Shel inexplicably, at breakneck speed, and I had so many unanswered questions. They made me so irrational. I didn't want to use God to explain it away like some people do (e.g., it was his time, or God works in mysterious ways), and I couldn't find the answers I needed on any medical report. He was just gone. I had to find a way to accept his death, because it was draining the life out of me to dwell on it. It wasn't enough, but this prayer by Reinhold Niebuhr became a mantra for me:

God grant me the serenity to accept the things I can't change; courage to change those things I can; and wisdom to know the difference.

My heart and soul will grieve for Shel for the rest of my days on Earth. All my efforts to understand what can't be understood in this life will haunt me until my own death. That will be the first thing I ask God in the next life:

Why did you take Shel from me?

CHAPTER 8:
DON'T FORGET TO SAY I LOVE YOU

*T*here are things I am grateful for when it comes to Shel. One of them is that we started saying "I love you" in the last two or three years of his life. We had reached that holy grail pinnacle in our relationship as siblings. We were adults and best friends. The big sister–little brother bickering fell away, and we became something quite special. We were peers and respected each other as individuals. We still teased each other, but we didn't argue anymore.

Shel and I had secret smiles that conveyed our thoughts to each other without our saying a word. We had started to realize we were companions in life. As survivors of a far-from-perfect childhood, we were apprehensively navigating our way through our twenties. We figuratively locked arms and started to skip down that yellow brick road of life. We settled in for the long haul and realized that when it came down to it, all we had was each other to get through.

There was an understanding we came to without saying a word to each other. One day we grew up and it was the best thing ever. He became more than my brother. I realized that there were two men in my life that knew me better than anyone: one was Brad and the other was Shel. I could strip down to the bare minimum that is me, in all my nasty glory, and I knew they would still love me.

The day I realized that I had that kind of love with Shel, we were on the phone. I had called for my parents, but they weren't there, so I chatted with Shel for a while. We talked easily and updated each other on our respective lives. We laughed and told jokes. We neared the end of the call, and I was so relaxed as I talked to him that I said, "I love you, Shel."

I surprised myself, because the sentence popped out of my mouth before I knew it. I felt weird for a second, like I'd let the cat out of the bag, and then I heard his deep voice say, "I love you too, Dee."

I smiled and said goodbye. After that it came easy. Every time we said goodbye, on the phone or in person, we said, "I love you." Those last few years of his life, when we said I love you and truly meant it, were such a gift. I know that Shel knew how I felt about him. People say it's such a girl thing to say "I love you" all the time. It's become such a *cliché*.

I know better.

Sometimes it is your last conversation with someone. It is a comfort to have said it out loud. Don't assume your loved one knows and doesn't need to hear it. I will never regret the times I said I love you. I regret the times I didn't say it. I wish I had said it more, but I'm content with the knowledge that I said it enough.

Some people see things as they are and ask why? I dream things that never were and ask why not?

—*Robert F. Kennedy*

CHAPTER 9:
MOVING ON

*A*fter Shel's funeral, I tried to return to my life. I came back to St. Paul and found myself in a new home. There were things to do that I didn't feel like doing. We had to wait for our furniture. We spent two weeks sitting on the floor, using blankets as cushions, waiting for our sofas to come. The TV was perched on a cardboard box. We had a bed to sleep on and not much else. Most of what I owned was back in North Dakota, and we weren't sure we wanted them anyway. An arrangement of plants and flowers came from the hospital for me. I was touched that my co-workers had cared enough to send them, and I cried. I unpacked things, I folded things, and I put them away in places I thought they belonged. I was on autopilot because things had to get done, but I wasn't fully there.

Shel is here with me.

His presence was everywhere. I could feel him. I entertained the idea that he was there in the house with me. Sometimes I would clean or get ready for the day, and I'd catch a glimpse in the mirror. A dark figure that was there and gone.

Was that Shel?

I didn't sleep much, and when I did, I had nightmares. Shel was dying. It was rarely in the way that he had died, but I always raced against the clock to save him. I was never successful. He died again and again. It was the same dream a million different ways, and I was always helpless to save him.

I did not like being alone. If Shel could die, I was not safe, either. If I got a headache, I would get scared. For a time, I was fearful that I might have contracted what he had. I didn't like it when Brad went to work, because I would hear noises in the house and be afraid. I was a quivering mess when I was alone. I was raw and completely exposed. I would close all the blinds and turn on the TV. I didn't like silence. I didn't like the darkness outside. Everything was a threat.

I was haunted.

My heart was in pieces in my chest. I cried much of the time, for several weeks. I called Brad at work. I tried to talk through it, to figure out what had happened. All I had to do was get him to Rochester. He would be okay if I got him to Rochester.

Why couldn't I save him?

Brad listened. He consoled. He was my rock. I was so weak with it. My Shel was gone.

I had wanted Shel to come and visit us. He would never see my house. There were trails down by St. Anthony Main that I knew he would love, and now I couldn't show them to him. I had wanted him to come to the Mall of America and explore it with me. There were a multitude of restaurants I wanted him to experience. I had fallen in love with the Twin Cities, and I knew he would have loved it as I did. I wanted him to understand why I had left everyone behind and made a life here. There were a thousand things I realized we would not be able to do. I would regain some composure, and then a new thought would occur to me, and I'd break down all over again.

One day, as I drove home from an errand, Shel's presence was in the car with me. There were so many times he had sat in the bucket seat next to me. My hands gripped the steering wheel in a death grip. I did not bother to choke back my sobs. There was a torrential downpour in that car, and I let myself be swept away by it.

"Shel, I know you're there," I said out loud, between sobs. "Wherever or whatever you are now, I love you. I believe you live on in the next life. Embrace where you are and where you're going, Shel. If there is somewhere you can go to be happy, go there with my blessing. It's okay to let go. I will always love you and I will always carry you with me. I want you to be happy, Shel."

A peace fell over the car as I fell silent. I let out a shuddering sigh and wiped away my tears. That day was a turning point for me. I wasn't haunted anymore. I stopped being so scared. I still missed him. That longing for him didn't wane. I thought of him every day.

I returned to work, and it was one of the hardest days of my life. It was not quite two weeks after Shel's death. A ball and chain of despair dragged at me as I entered the hospital. I walked through the PICU doors and saw my co-workers and willed myself to be strong.

"We were so sorry to hear about your brother . . ."

"You've been in my prayers . . ."

"Hang in there, Dee . . . time will heal the pain."

I received several hugs before I reached my desk at the front of the unit. I was holding it together. I saw Michelle, my fellow unit coordinator and friend. She smiled at me, and I returned her smile.

"I am so sorry for your loss," she said. She placed her hand over mine. "How old was your brother?"

"Twenty-seven," my voice cracked. The tears came right behind.

I sobbed at the front desk. My story spilled out. I would tell it many times. Everyone knew what had happened. There was a mixture of curiosity and sympathy. I bent the ears of many nurses and staff. I will never forget their kindness. It was therapeutic working there. The flow of my tears eased with each time I told the story.

I was not myself. In the movie *Sleepless in Seattle*, Tom Hanks' character talks about the loss of his wife. He had to remind himself to breathe in and out and to get out of bed every morning. It really was like that for me for a while. The loss of Shel was like quicksand. The more I tried to crawl out of my grief, the more I became mired in it.

About a month after Shel died, I wound up in a doctor's office. I was depressed, anxious, and not sleeping well. The doctor gave me some anti-depressants. He referred me to a psychiatrist. I made an appointment but couldn't bring myself to go—it just wasn't the way I was raised. I was taught to be strong and handle things on my own. I took the pills until they were gone but didn't bother with a refill. They erased feelings I probably needed to endure. Maybe I would be a wreck for a while. I decided that would have to be okay. As tough as the going would be, I decided to face it myself.

What bothered me the most was that we would not grow old together. I had plans for us. I was excited that Shel would finally be moving out of Mom and Dad's. When his birthday came on November 29, he would get his next cash settlement. He had not had a seizure in two years, and he could finally get his driver's license back.

Mom told him they would help him find a car and an apartment. He would most likely live in Steele, so that Shannon and his family would be nearby. I was overjoyed that he would finally have his freedom. Unfortunate circumstances had kept him from being able to go out into the world on his own. This would be *his* time.

He would probably meet a girl in Steele. They would fall in love, and he would marry her. By the time he did that, Brad and I would be married, too. Shel would have kids and I would have kids, and we'd watch them grow up together. Our children would play together. I'd look over at Shel and we would smile.

There was a fantasy life that I had been tenderly weaving in my mind somewhere. A glimpse into a happy future that was inevitable. Shel deserved that life. Sometimes I still can't wrap my mind around the fact that he won't have that life.

He'll always be twenty-seven, single, and a great uncle who should have had kids himself. I wanted so much more for him. I tell myself he's happy now, at peace, but sometimes that's not enough and I want him back. I will miss him for the rest of my life.

There was a guestbook attached to his online obituary. I viewed people's entries, and I was deeply touched. I paid to have the obituary online for a full year. I figured people would find out about his death later and I wanted them to have the option to leave a message.

I added an entry thanking everyone for the kind words they had said. The messages stopped, but I still would go visit his guestbook. His birthday came and I wrote him a note. I told him I was celebrating his life and that I loved him.

After that, the guestbook became my journal. I didn't intend for it to be that way, but I would go to the guestbook to talk to him. I told him what was going on in my life. It was therapeutic to have a place to go with my thoughts. I didn't care that it wasn't meant to be my journal. I needed a place to go with it all. The guestbook was a blessing for me.

Several months passed and I began to heal. There were times I would drive home at night and walk in the door crying. Brad knew without words what was wrong and would hold me until I pulled away.

The bad nights became fewer and farther between. The nightmares weren't as frequent. I had a couple of dreams where things were normal and we were a complete family again. I'd wake up with the most bittersweet smile on my lips. I was sad to wake up, but happy that I'd seen Shel as I wanted to remember him.

I picked up my life again and went back to school. Work was never quite the same, but I didn't see how it could be. I saw my sadness reflected in the families that came into the PICU and it got hard sometimes. The PICU staff was a blessing during those times. They knew how to shepherd someone through the grieving process, and they propped me up when I needed help.

I began to realize that Shel would want me to move on. I took steps toward living life again. It was a different life, and I was a different person, but I tried to make the best of it.

CHAPTER 10:
CHRISTMAS IN MINNESOTA

I decided to invite my parents down to our house for Christmas. I knew their house wouldn't be the same and I wanted to provide some respite for them. It was like getting three hard punches to the gut. There was Thanksgiving. Then Shel's birthday came on November 29. So, we needed a different kind of Christmas. I hoped to make the third punch a little less noticeable.

I was surprised when they agreed to come. I was in a flurry getting the house ready. This was our first Christmas without Shel, and I wanted them to like my new home. I bought as many Christmas decorations as I could with a new mortgage payment looming overhead. I did my best to make everything cozy and comfortable. I wanted everything to be just right.

Another package arrived one day, and Brad retrieved it with a sigh. "Dee," he said softly. He waited until my eyes met his. "This is enough. Stop ordering stuff. Your parents are coming to see you, not Christmas decorations."

I nodded and realized he was right. I was going overboard, trying to make up for their son being gone.

Before I knew it, the evening before Christmas Eve arrived. They were running quite late, which worried me. My parents were not the best navigators.

I called Shannon. "Do you know where Mom and Dad are?" I asked him.

"Not a clue," he said. "Hold on, I'll conference them into this call."

"Hello," Dad answered the phone, sounding mildly annoyed.

"Hey, Dad," Shannon responded, "I've got Dee on the line. Where are you guys at?"

"We're on 35W North," he explained.

"Dad, what was the last exit you saw?" I asked.

"Highway 96," he responded.

"Great! You're almost here. Look for exit 123; it's coming," I assured him.

"35W doesn't make sense when it runs north," Dad pointed out.

I laughed. I had the same thought when I moved to the Twin Cities. "I know. It's weird. But think of it as just a W, not west," I explained.

"How has the trip been so far?" Shannon asked.

"Some snow and sleet, but nothing too bad," Dad responded. "This is the exit, Judi."

"When you come off the ramp, take a left," I instructed. I heard him relay what I said to Mom, then he said, "Done. What next?"

"Go until you hit the stop sign. You'll see a Shell gas station. Take a right. You'll see a bunch of townhomes. Go to the second entrance and take a right. Then take a left and another right. We're 2095, in the middle of the street."

I could hear him giving instructions to Mom. Then they were in our driveway.

"I see you! I think we're good, Shannon. Thanks for the con-call," I said with a laugh.

"No problem!" Shannon said. He sounded relieved. "Hope you guys have fun."

We all hung up.

I could see my parents grab their bags from the car. I opened my arms to them as they walked through the door. It was so good to see them.

Shel's absence was weird. It was like one of the three stooges was missing. I covered my sadness with a smile. I gave them a tour of the new house as a distraction. We got them settled into the guest room. We had a nice, relaxing night catching up before we finally went to bed.

I had a few things planned for their visit, though I was a little limited by the weather. Winter didn't afford many options for fun things to do with your parents, but I made the best of it.

I took them to Pracna, a trendy little eatery down by St. Anthony's Main. It was far from its full glory, but we could see the icy river and the buildings downtown. It was the epitome of a downtown Minneapolis restaurant. The food was great, conversation was easy, and I could tell they liked the place.

Then something happened that I will never forget. My Dad ordered a beer.

Let me rephrase: My *recovering* alcoholic father ordered a beer. Doctors had told my father that he would die if he started drinking again.

I sprang on him like a spider monkey. "Dad, what are you doing?" I asked him in a stern tone. I wanted to scream at him, but I didn't want to make a scene.

"It's only one beer," he replied in a low voice. "I know what I'm doing."

"Dad, you know you're not supposed to drink," I hissed between my teeth.

He averted his gaze. In a quiet voice, he said, "Just because I can't drink like I used to doesn't mean that I can't ever have a beer."

I fell silent and looked down at my plate. I shook my head. I had an uneasy feeling that I couldn't quite shake. Dad changed the subject, and I let it go.

That night we had dinner at Buca di Beppo, an Italian restaurant that I love in St. Paul. It was always bustling with activity. There was richly colored decor, beautiful woodwork throughout, and Christmas lights that stayed up all year. The food was fantastic. I knew Mom and Dad would like it, especially Dad. I had always wanted to take him there because of the music. Dean Martin and Frank Sinatra, two of his favorite musicians, were played frequently there.

It was nice to be part of a couple with my parents present. That was new for me. I was grateful that Brad seemed comfortable with them. I could tell my parents liked him too, which was important to me. I didn't need their permission, but it was a comfort to know they approved of him.

Buca serves their fare family style, so Brad and I ordered our favorites for the table to share. Once again, my dad ordered a beer. I was perplexed and disappointed with him. My boyfriend liked a drink as much as the next guy, but he had refrained so that my dad wouldn't be tempted. It was a deep betrayal to hear him order another beer in front of me.

"Dad, what's going on?" I asked as I bent toward him across the table.

"It's not a big deal," he replied as he met my gaze. "You have nothing to worry about. I'm fine."

I sat back in my chair and took a deep breath. I looked away. What could I do? Throw a tantrum? Take the beer and whip it across the room in my frustration? I did none of these things. It was a helpless feeling and I prayed that these were isolated incidents. Maybe Dad was just enjoying himself during a visit to the Twin Cities. I hoped beyond hope that it was nothing more than that.

We had a nice relaxing dinner together. The food did not disappoint, and my parents were happy with the meal and the atmosphere of the place. Dad got up and gave himself a tour of the place. He liked the pictures of famous Italians hanging on the walls. To my chagrin, the din of the restaurant prevented us from hearing the music, which Dad would have enjoyed the most. I still considered it a success. Dad only drank half of his beer. Maybe I had overreacted.

The next day was Christmas Eve. I treated my parents to a trip to downtown Minneapolis. My father had known a younger Minneapolis from visits when he was in his twenties. I wanted him to see all the changes that had occurred since then. He was highly impressed, as was Mom.

I beamed as I showed them the city I had come to love and enjoy. It was a city that kept me farther from them than they liked. I wanted to show them a smattering of what I found appealing, by way of explanation. They were in awe of the tall buildings and the architecture, the various window displays, the people, and the vibe. My parents seemed to like what they saw, which pleased me.

I brought them to my place of work. I wanted them to see the place where I helped save lives. I introduced them to some of the nurses and showed them where I sat during my shifts. I gave them a mini tour of the PICU.

My dad looked a little apprehensive. He pulled me aside and whispered, "Some of these children already look dead."

I huddled in between him and Mom and whispered back, "These kids are gravely ill. Some of them have cancer or severe heart defects. But I work with some fantastic doctors, and I see miracles every day."

My parents nodded, their expressions grave. I could tell they were proud of me and my decision to become a nurse. I was showing them pieces of me; I wanted them to understand why I had moved away from them to find a life of my own.

I drove them to the college I attended. I had saved the best for last. The college is next to the Basilica of Saint Mary. It is a grand, stately Catholic Church that I have loved since first sight. I am so in love with it that I've considered converting to Catholicism. The enormity of it, the beauty, takes my breath away every time.

I had first seen the sanctuary decorated for Easter. There were pastel-colored ribbons strewn across the room, with the intricate woodwork gleaming, daylight streaming through the enormous stained-glass windows. The room was bathed in color and light. I was awestruck by its beauty.

It was now decorated for Christmas. Red, gold, and green decorations were on every pew, the pulpit decked out in poinsettia splendor. There were evergreen trees that were thirty feet tall sprinkled throughout the church, their clear lights twinkling brightly. There was a service that night that we intruded on, but we blended in, and my parents enjoyed the hustle and bustle of the parishioners. The only drawback was that we didn't feel we could linger too long and look at everything. Regardless, I am so glad I took them there. My parents marveled at the beautiful stained-glass windows and architecture. Children laughed and scampered about, which made Dad chuckle to himself. There was jubilance in the air, an extraordinary spirit that was contagious, and I was tempted to stay for the service. Instead, we went on our way.

We walked for a block; there was more I wanted them to see, but Dad said he was getting tired. The brisk air was too cold for his lungs, and his sinuses were giving him trouble. We went back to the car, and I drove them home. We rested until Brad got home from work, and then we all had dinner. Afterward, we drove to the Minnesota Museum of Science; we had tickets to a show in the Omni Theater there.

The Omni Theater is a one-of-a-kind experience. It is a generous dome-shaped screen that curves around stadium seating. It caters to the senses and it's impossible to not become engrossed in the show. I knew my parents would love it.

We saw a film about the Nile River, and they were impressed by how the vast shape of the screen made the movie seem so real. My dad particularly enjoyed it. He liked that it was informational as well as entertaining. Dad didn't like frivolous movies. He was not one for science fiction or fantasy; he liked movies that told a story that could be true or was true. I hit the nail on the head by taking him to that show. Mom was happy with most anything I planned for them, but Dad was a little harder to please.

Christmas came the next morning. Mom made Christmas dinner for us, including a turkey, mashed potatoes and gravy, our family's famous green beans, dressing, a pumpkin pie, and an apple pie. She was appalled that I had no rolling pin, so Brad and I picked one up the day before, along with a few other things she needed. Mom and I stayed in the kitchen and prepared the meal, while the men watched football on TV. I didn't mind at all; I wanted Dad and Brad to have time to bond.

We sat down to a nice lunch a little after noon. I set the dining room table for four, which was a treat, since Brad and I usually ate at the eat-in kitchen counter. We had a delicious meal and stuffed ourselves. We snacked throughout the afternoon and watched Christmas movies.

That evening, it was time to open gifts. I sucked in a deep breath, hoping my parents would like the present I made for them.

I opened the gift from them first. It was a sheet and comforter set for our new king-sized bed. I was thrilled, since we didn't have extra sheets yet. I complained to Mom about it once, which was all it took. Mom was so good about that kind of thing. I wouldn't necessarily have to ask her for something; she would remember something I'd said, and come Christmas or birthday time, what I had wanted (within reason) was mine.

I had bought them a DVD player the previous Christmas, so their first gift was a DVD collection of Clint Eastwood movies I knew they would enjoy (*The Outlaw Josey Wales* was one of their favorites). The second gift was the one that made me nervous—I had composed a poem about Shel, printed it on stationery paper, and framed it. The poem follows:

Grieve Not

Grieve not for me
And please don't cry
Or call my name in vain
There's no sense wondering why
Things just can't be the same
For I had to answer His call
You see I met my Savior today
"I've been waiting for you, Shel Wahl"
He said, with the warmth of a summer day,
And He held my hand in His own
As we crossed a crystal sea
He explained in detail the life I had sewn
How He'd kept his eyes on me
I asked why I had to leave you
And he replied patiently
That I'd done what I had come to do
Someday everyone would see
That His plan is for us to love one another
And no one loves us more than He
I learned my lesson young
Twenty-seven years was enough for me
And while His will had to be done
I think you would agree
I loved, I laughed, I lived my life
And I've met my destiny;
For reflected in my Father's eyes
Is all the love I need
Made all the more sweeter
By the love I brought with me

My father opened the gift, read a couple of lines, and wordlessly handed it to my mother. He went downstairs in silence. His reaction made me mentally flinch, and I wondered if I had made a mistake.

Mom read it and cried, which made me cry.

"It's so beautiful, Dee," she said softly as we hugged. "Thank you so much."

"You're welcome, Mom," I said, my arms still wrapped around her. "I love you."

"I love you too, baby." We parted and began to clean up the discarded Christmas wrapping.

Dad said nothing to me about the poem during their stay. At the time I was hurt; I thought he didn't like it. Dad told me later that he had liked it very much. He just didn't want to break down in front of us on Christmas. He wanted to read it later in private. He hadn't realized how good I was at writing poems. To hear that affirmation from him meant more than I could say. That poem was therapy for me. I had given it to them with the hope that it would comfort them, as writing it had comforted me.

After the gift opening, we watched *Miracle on 34th Street*, which is one of my favorite Christmas movies. I adored Maureen O'Hara as an actress, and Natalie Wood was so perfect in it. The fireplace was on, and we were drinking hot chocolate and tea. Mom's pies were a hit. We lounged on the sofas in the living room, swathed in fleecy blankets, with our bellies full. We chatted the whole evening, and for the first time in a while, I was content to live in the moment.

It still felt like Shel was in the next room and would walk in at any moment. He was noticeably absent; I missed him like crazy. But I don't think Christmas was as painful as it could have been for us. It was wise to ask my parents to come and visit me instead of going home to Tuttle. Christmas in Minnesota had masked our pain a little bit, and things had gone as well as could be expected.

CHAPTER 11:
THE NEW YEAR

I was a mess on New Year's Eve. It was horrible to know I was leaving 2005 behind after losing Shel. I was starting a new year without him, and the pain was palpable. I held a glass of bubbly champagne and looked over at Brad with tears streaming down my face. We had a long hug and I mused about the gamut of feelings that assaulted me. In one sense I was so devastated, and in another, I clung to the hope that life might return to some semblance of order. I had hope that while things would never be the same, life would still regain meaning for me. Some days I wondered if it ever would.

I could never go back to the person I was, but I had hope that the person I was now would persevere. Three months into my grief, it seemed like a very tall order.

Nevertheless, when the New Year's ball dropped at Times Square, I kissed my boyfriend and threw my arms around him.

I made a toast to Shel. "To Shel, the best brother I could have hoped for. I love you, buddy. I celebrate you tonight."

We clinked our glasses and kissed again.

I hoped that a new year would mean a new beginning.

Shel would want me to be happy.

I vowed that I would try to be happy for him, until I could be happy for myself.

CHAPTER 12:
GRANDPA JERRY

My cell phone rang in the middle of the night in mid-March. The call was from my mother. My Grandpa Jerry, my mother's father, had died. I started to cry as she told me. I cried for my mother; she had lost her son and now she had lost her father. Her heartache traveled from her phone to mine, and I was very sad for her.

The truth was I didn't know the man. He was a wispy figure in my life at best. It's always sad to hear that someone has lost their life, but most of my emotions were not for me. My mother had been close to him and that was enough. She had lost my grandmother, Jane, years ago, when I was nineteen. Her stepmother, Carmen, had died three years before. Grandpa Jerry was the last parent Mom lost. While he had been ill and had lived out his life at age eighty-three, it was still a heartbreaking loss. The timing couldn't have been worse.

My parents went to stay at Grandpa Jerry's house. They used the money they found in Grandpa Jerry's bureau to fly Brad and me to Reno, Nevada, for the funeral. My brothers tried their best to come too, but flights from North Dakota to Nevada were not as easy to come by. They would not be able to make it until after the funeral had passed. Unfortunately, Brad and I would have to fly home before they arrived.

I packed my pearl-gray suit—oh, that poor suit! I had hoped to wear it somewhere nice sometime, a restaurant perhaps, or maybe to a show. Instead, it was serving as funeral garb once again. I booked our flights through Priceline and received a discount. The downside was we would have plenty of layovers. I would learn what a mistake that would be later.

We arrived in Reno at about 8:00 p.m., two nights before the funeral. My parents looked well, considering the circumstances. They were glad to see us. We went back to Grandpa Jerry's house and visited for a while. Then Brad and I retired for the evening.

My parents did not advertise Grandpa Jerry's death in the newspaper at all.

"Why not, Mom?" I asked with a frown. "Don't you think people have a right to know?"

"No," my mother said flatly. "I let his neighbors know about the service. They are the only ones that need to know. They were like family to him."

"But Mom, what if there are other people that want to pay their respects?" I tried again.

"I don't want the general public to know," she said as she resolutely met my gaze. "Your Grandpa Jerry was a wealthy man. I'm leery of people taking advantage of the situation. It happened to me when my mother died, and it's not going to happen with my dad."

I gave up; she had obviously made up her mind. I didn't agree with her, but it was her dad. I was there to support her, so I had to respect her wishes.

We did have some fun on the trip. Brad and I did some light gambling at a couple of casinos one night. We went to lunch with Mom and Dad the next day. We were seated and looked at our menus. It was a steak and potato joint.

"I want to eat something light," I said to the table. "I feel like I haven't eaten the healthiest in the last couple of days. I think I'll have the taco salad."

The waiter came to our table, and we placed our orders. Everyone else ordered steaks, but I was proud to have gone the healthy route.

The wait staff brought our food to the table. I couldn't believe my taco salad. "Will you look at this monstrosity?" I exclaimed, and everyone started laughing.

"That's a nice, light lunch you have there," Dad sputtered out, shaking with laughter.

The toasty tortilla shell was huge and overflowing with a waterfall of taco fixings. It was a masterpiece to be sure, but three of me couldn't have eaten all that food! Brad took a picture of it with his camera phone. I did my best with it but could only consume half of it.

It was my first time in Reno, as well as Brad's. I loved the mountains that surrounded my grandfather's home. At first, I had mistaken them for clouds and then realized they were mountains. There were a multitude of stores and shops, but I didn't think it was all that different from St. Paul. The real difference was the weather. In St. Paul, the snow was a constant in the winter. In Reno, it would snow in the morning, but it was gone by the afternoon; the sun shining brightly. Reno was lovely; I could see why Jerry liked it, but I decided I would miss the Minnesota lakes too much.

I got a kick out of Grandpa Jerry and Grandma Carmen's house. They had done nothing to update it through the years. Apparently, the seventies were their favorite decade, because their home looked like it still resided there. When I stepped into the house, it was literally like stepping back in time thirty years. I worried about its marketability when it came time to sell.

I saw glimpses of a life that must have been happy. It was obvious that he loved Grandma Carmen very much. On a polaroid snapshot of her, he had scrawled the words, "I love you, honey. I miss your beautiful smile." My eyes swam with tears as I read it. I really hadn't known him at all. I had called him once or twice as an adult. I sent him a Christmas card after Carmen's passing. But he had never seemed interested in getting to know me, and I couldn't figure out why.

Mom told me Grandpa Jerry had been hurt by his mother-in-law. He had been overseas, serving as a merchant marine. My grandmother, Jane, divorced Grandpa Jerry when Mom was three because he was gone so much. He regularly sent money for my mother's care, but Grandma Jane did not receive it. She scraped by under my great-grandmother's grudging charity, oblivious that the woman was intercepting her mail and stealing money from her. Eventually, Grandma Jane became fed up with her mother's ill-treatment and moved in with a friend until she could afford her own place.

Grandma Jane died thinking my grandfather hadn't cared enough to support her and their child. Mom and Grandpa Jerry had been estranged for several years before they reconnected and the truth about everything came out. Mom cited this as the reason he was skittish about being involved with family. I didn't buy it; nothing that happened back then was his grandchildren's fault. It was an excuse for his behavior, and it didn't help me understand anything. He would talk to me if I called him. He sent me a Christmas card after I sent him one. He did the minimum required. I wanted him to want to know me, but he never did. Nor did he keep in contact with my brothers. Now he was gone and all I had were mementos—notes, books, magazines, paintings, and furniture; his things were all that were left for me. I knew he had stories to tell me—great stories of places he had traveled, people he had met and loved. I would never hear them now.

I went around the house and claimed things. Mom told me to write my name on the things I wanted, and I went a little crazy. It became a joke between my brothers. When they came to visit later, they saw various things adorned with masking tape that had my little name on it. I was a little over-zealous because I had a house now. I had a place to put things. I was such a nomad before we bought the house. Everything I inherited had to go into storage. I was always someone's roommate, or I had an apartment with limited room. It was nice to know I had my own home to decorate now.

Ironically, I returned home to find that the things I picked out wouldn't work in our house; we already had our own style. Some of Grandpa Jerry's things were unorthodox. There were huge, elephant-shaped plant holders, elaborate Asian vases, and gaudy lamps that would look great in a burlesque house. These were things he had purchased as he travelled the globe. While I was at his house, I found some of them charming. When I got home, I realized they wouldn't suit the modern look of our house.

All my life I had heard of his wealth. I expected a palace. What I found was a seventies-style house full of Grandpa Jerry's sentimental belongings and not much else. The furniture was nice, but there was nothing of *real* value in my eyes. These things had been priceless to him, but I didn't have any emotional ties to any of it. There wasn't a watch that I remembered him wearing or a sweater I knew he liked. I didn't know where he had traveled to purchase these things. My mother scarcely knew. I was a stranger in my grandfather's house.

Grandpa Jerry's funeral was held on a bitterly cold day. It was sunny with bright blue skies, but when I stepped outside, the wind cut me to the bone. I was dressed in my pearl-gray suit and some heels. I wore a warm coat and gloves. There was a flurry around the house as we readied ourselves. We arrived at the church and sat in the front pew.

It was a closed casket—I was grateful for that. I knew him from pictures, and I didn't want this to be my last impression of him. I sat by my mother and cried because she did. Grandpa Jerry hadn't been there for much of her life. Fifteen years prior to his death, she had called him. They slowly got to know each other. During their visits, they realized that many of her mannerisms were the same as his. He hadn't raised her, but she was obviously his child. She had his eyes and spoke in the same cadence he did. I knew fifteen years hadn't been enough for her.

I put my arm around Mom and held her hand. I tried to comfort her. She held her funeral program over her face to hide her sobs.

There were very few people in the pews. Only Grandpa Jerry's neighbors were there. I heard some of them crying. How strange it was that his neighbors knew him better than I ever would.

Because he had served his country, *taps* was played on bagpipes by a young marine that was a neighbor of Grandpa Jerry's. It was a military memorial, very stoic and solemn. Some of the neighbors stood up and told a couple of stories about Grandpa. I recognized one of them; Doe, a close friend of Grandpa's, was there. She said a poem that touched me greatly. I knew her because she had been kind to my mother. She had made some phone calls and had stopped over to visit with my parents a few times. She was a tall, attractive woman in her seventies. She had a commanding presence and I liked her immediately. Doe was the kind of woman you wanted in your corner.

The funeral home attendants tried to get out of doing the graveside service, citing the weather. I was amused, as it was lightly snowing outside, with some wind. It was nothing some northerners couldn't handle. I was about to protest, but Doe was a step ahead of me.

"His grandchildren are flying back to Minnesota tomorrow morning," she said to the man. "We need you to do the graveside service now."

"But ma'am . . .," he began to protest.

"There is no reason you can't do the service now," she said haughtily. She peered down her patrician nose at him. "Wear a coat."

"Yes, ma'am," he relented.

We trooped out to the graveside. We threw in flowers and said a prayer.

Doe stepped in to comfort my mother. "I knew your dad when he was forty-five years old," she said softly. "He had just bought his house. He was young and handsome, and so full of life. I greatly enjoyed knowing him and will miss him dearly."

I watched them embrace. I wished I had known Grandpa Jerry even a fraction as much as Doe. I held Brad's hand and we walked to the car. I hoped it would be a long time before I had to go to another funeral.

We lazed about the rest of the day. We went out and had a nice dinner at a buffet restaurant in my grandfather's favorite casino, The Peppermill. I treated my parents and paid far too much. I made one negative comment and sent Dad off on a rampage. One thing Dad liked to do was complain. I could tell Brad was uncomfortable, so I intervened and soothed my father. He relented and we had a nice time. The buffet really did have every kind of food imaginable. We had a nice, relaxing meal that salvaged the day somewhat. Mom seemed to be taking everything in stride, for which I was grateful.

Brad and I flew out the next day and began what would turn into a nightmarish trip home. In an effort to keep down costs, we were subjected to two layovers. As tired as we were, the delay was excruciating.

The first layover was in Las Vegas, which intrigued Brad, since he had never been there. I hadn't been there since I was eighteen. We both looked out the windows longingly. We mused about how nice it would be to stay for the night. The layover wasn't long enough to do anything more than hang out at the airport.

The next layover was for three hours in Denver, which seemed like a lifetime to us. We had a bite to eat and waited out the time with as much grace as we could muster. I made a vow to never accept layovers again. No discount is worth the trouble.

We tried to make the best of it. The last leg of the flight was in the late evening in a small plane. It was a turbulent flight that jarred my frazzled nerves. I snuggled with one of the small pillows the flight attendants had provided and talked with Brad about our trip.

Brad noticed the same thing I did—my dad was drinking again. He tried to be furtive about it, but we both noticed it. I was apprehensive that my parents had decided to extend their stay in Reno. I worried that Dad would become a drunkard again, that he would drown his sorrow over the loss of Shel. He was now armed with Grandpa Jerry's wealth.

My tired mind couldn't grapple with our discovery. I knew I couldn't make Dad stop drinking. I couldn't believe he had turned to alcohol yet again.

Just then I looked out the plane window and saw the lights of the Twin Cities loom up ahead. I decided Dad's drinking was a problem for another day. After we arrived at the airport, we wearily grabbed our bags, drove home, and went to bed.

There's no way around grief and loss; you can dodge all you want, but sooner or later, you just have to go into it, through it, and hopefully come out the other side. The world you find there will never be the same as the world you left.

—Johnny Cash

CHAPTER 13:

HIS GRIEF

There was not much that Grandpa Jerry left for me in the way of life lessons, but I learned at least one from him. After his death, the truth started to come out. I heard horrible things I wouldn't want to hear about anyone, let alone my grandfather. Mom had been in contact with his brother Jim. Jim had tried to keep an eye on Grandpa since Carmen's death, but it proved to be more of a job than he anticipated. He would come to see Grandpa, and his house would look like a cyclone had hit it. Grandma Carmen had cooked his meals for him. After her death, Grandpa had relied on fast food from KFC and dinners at the nearby Peppermill casino. Jim tried to do what he could, but he couldn't make his brother want to live. He felt helpless when Grandpa ignored his efforts to get him some help.

The breaking point came in March of 2006. Jim came to see Grandpa on one of his periodic visits. He found that one of Grandpa and Grandma's long-time pets, a standard poodle, had died. The odd thing was that it had died in Grandpa's living room, and he had not bothered to remove the dog. It had started to decompose where it had dropped dead. Jim buried the dog and did what he could to clean up Grandpa's house.

It was clear to Jim that Grandpa had given up. His house was a complete disaster, and he could hardly walk. After Jim took him to the hospital, it was found that Grandpa had a foot infection and it had turned gangrenous. He had also been diagnosed with colon cancer, which had gone untreated. Jim pleaded with Grandpa to go to the hospital and Grandpa finally relented. Amid the stress of caring for Grandpa, Jim had a minor stroke himself.

Grandpa died a couple of weeks after Jim's discovery of his dire situation. Mom found out later that Grandpa hadn't paid his taxes in three years. She had to deal with the consequences of his actions herself.

I barely knew the man, but the terrible circumstances of his final days haunted me. His heartbreak after Grandma Carmen's death must have been excruciating, and he had faced it all alone. In the three years since her death, he had spiraled into a complete collapse that resulted in the loss of his own life.

If only he had contacted Mom at some point; we would have made sure that he received the proper care. I would have jumped at the chance to know him and be a comfort to him. I was saddened that my grandfather didn't care or trust anyone enough to ask for help. I hoped that he had finally found peace at last.

I resolved to never give up on life as he had done. No matter the losses I faced, I would choose life. I could not have dreamed it at that point in time, but one day it would come to that for me.

CHAPTER 14:
THE SPIRAL

here were signs along the way that let me know Dad was in trouble. I noticed some of them while he stayed with us for Christmas. They were little things—he forgot where he left the remote or that he had already told me a story. Brad and I also noticed that he would miss the rim of our toilet when he urinated. This is certainly not unusual for men, but it looked like he hadn't even aimed. I didn't give these things much thought at the time; I attributed most of it to his age.

After Grandpa Jerry died, my parents lived in his house for months. I talked to them on the phone, and sometimes Dad sounded like he'd had a few. He began to worsen, and my brothers and I became concerned. We realized that our mother was his enabler, because she didn't have the capacity to stand up to him.

Dad didn't like to be told what to do by anyone, least of all our mother. He would wear her down and berate her. During our phone calls, I learned that there was a bar they frequented to have meals and a *few* drinks. My mother admitted to me that Dad was indeed drinking again. She didn't seem overly concerned, or perhaps felt helpless to do anything about it. She made excuses for his behavior.

In May, I came back to Bismarck for a visit. We got together as a family at Shad's house. It was strange that our parents were not in attendance. The kids were on a huge trampoline without Shel, which was terribly odd. It seemed like we were in a covert meeting and had forgotten to invite them.

Since I lived in Minnesota, I was often not aware of things going on in my own family. My sisters-in-law caught me up while the men played horseshoes. My parents wanted to stay in Reno longer, but we couldn't think of a reason that they needed to be there. Grandpa Jerry's estate had to be in order by now, given that my parents had been there since March. Mom had tried to pack up some of his things, but she quit when she realized that Dad wasn't going to help her. It sounded like they were there to have a good time rather than accomplish anything useful. We decided that we needed to apply some serious pressure to get them to return home. We feared that Dad was worse than Mom had told us. We wanted them back home so we could monitor his condition.

It was a sunny day with puffy white clouds hugging a blue sky, the wind a reminder that we were still in ND. Here we were, the three surviving siblings, with our significant others. The kids played in the background. I waited for Shel to come around the corner. Dad usually threw horseshoes with the boys. My boyfriend played in his place, and Cole played instead of Shel. It was a peculiar shuffle and a reminder that life had moved on after Shel's death. I glimpsed a future where our parents would not be there. It occurred to me again that nothing was within our control. We could talk and plan, but I had an eerie feeling that our future had already been set in motion and there was nothing we could do to stop it.

We somehow managed to talk our parents into coming back home by June. I talked to Shannon on the phone a few times in the meantime.

"Dad's not doing well," he said in defeat.

"What's going on?" I asked. I wondered if he knew something I didn't.

"I can just tell that he's drinking more than he should, and Mom can't be trusted to keep him in line at all," he said sadly.

"I can't believe we're here again," I said with resignation.

"I know. Sometimes I think we should put him in West Central again, for ninety days this time," he hedged.

"We'd need another court order, and Mom said she'd never do it again because Dad was so angry about it last time," I said. I didn't want to discourage Shannon, but Dad going in again was a long shot. "Mom is just so brainwashed, or maybe just tired."

"She seems to be doing more harm than good at this point," he agreed.

"I think West Central would just delay the same behavior. He must want help and he doesn't. He is choosing booze, even though doctors have said it will kill him," I said in frustration.

Then Shannon said something that would always stick with me.

"That is the whole problem. We can't make him get the help he needs. We can't make him want this, which makes me feel helpless. I know that someday I'm going to get a phone call. I'm going to get a call and the person on the line is going to tell me that Dad is dead. It won't be a big surprise, and I know I'll feel like I didn't do enough, even though that won't be true. I try to prepare myself for that call, because I know it's coming someday. And it will be a day that comes too soon, but there will be nothing I can do about it. He will have made his choice, and I will have to live with it."

We hung up. Nothing would be decided by our calls. We were beating our heads against a brick wall. Ultimately, I realized the calls were more about commiseration than anything else.

The month of July was an emotional jumble for me. My grandmother was turning ninety on the tenth, and the family had planned a birthday party for her. It sounded like it would be more of a reunion because *everybody* was going to be there.

Everybody except me.

We were behind on bills and living paycheck-to-paycheck. I couldn't spend the money needed for a trip back to Bismarck. I explained the situation to Dad.

"Do you think Grandma will be upset?" I asked him with desperation.

"No, she'll understand. Don't worry about it," he soothed me.

"I feel so bad, Dad. She's turning ninety and I'm not going to be there," I said with a sob in my throat.

"You were just here in May, honey. It'll be okay," he said softly.

Dad never offered to help foot the bill for our trip, which was the only way we could have made it. I had too much pride to ask him for help. I had to miss it, which broke my heart, because it was an important birthday for her. Dad said he would talk to her for me.

I called Grandma to wish her a happy birthday later.

"Happy birthday, Grandma! I love you so much!" I shouted into the phone.

"Well, thank you so much!" she said happily.

"I am so sorry to miss your party," I said forlornly.

"DeeDee, it is fine. I just saw you in May! And there will be so many people there. I'm afraid I won't be able to spend as much time with people as I'd like to," she said gently.

We talked for a few more minutes and then said goodbye.

I found out later that everyone had a grand time without me. People that no one had seen in years showed up. Everyone posed for about a million pictures, laughed, and reminisced. It was the reunion I had known it would be. I deeply regretted my absence, but I was glad so many people had been there. Grandma had a fabulous day where she felt loved and appreciated, and that was all that really mattered.

Later that month, Dad showed me his true colors.

I wanted a dog. Brad didn't want pets for the first year after we moved into the new house, but I was so lonely. It had been nine months since we'd moved in, and I had become resentful of Brad's refusal to let me buy a dog. I hatched a plan to get one on my own.

I wanted a puggle (a pug crossed with a beagle), because I had seen some puggles on *The Today Show*. I fell in love with their looks and personality. Something was driving me that I can't even explain. I wrote out a check for $100. I purposefully strode to our mailbox, envelope in hand, and pushed it through the outgoing mail slot. I had just mailed a deposit to the breeder. I sighed deeply and wondered what I had done. For the first time, I had deliberately done something that Brad had expressly forbidden me to do.

He had not made an outrageous request; a year was a reasonable time to wait before bringing a pet into our home. I just couldn't help myself. I was obsessed. I wanted some puppy joy to ease my pain. The thought of having that furry comfort made my common sense fly out the window. I was willing to risk Brad's anger to find a little peace. For some reason, I figured a goofy little puppy would make things better.

I needed some financial help, because puggles were not cheap. I had to pick up the dog by the end of July and I only had half of the money I needed. I decided to ask my mother for the rest. I was a little embarrassed to ask her, but I knew she would help me get one. I had no pride. All I could think about was getting this dog.

I called her on the way home from work one day.

"Hello?" she answered after a couple of rings.

"Hi, Mom," I said tentatively. "Do you have time to talk?"

"Sure," she said.

"Well, I have a bit of a problem. I really want to get a dog. I think it would help with my grief, and I just can't stop thinking about it. Brad doesn't want a dog right now, so I don't want to ask him for money to get one. I'm hoping he'll come around after I bring the puppy home. I have half of what I need to buy her. Can you help me with the rest?" I asked hopefully.

"How much do you need?" she asked me.

"Two hundred and fifty dollars," I said softly. "I already put down a deposit on her and I can bring her home at the end of this month."

"Sure," Mom said, "not a problem. I'll get a check in the mail for you tomorrow."

"Thanks so much, Mom!" I said joyfully into the phone. "I can't even tell you how happy this makes me!"

"Sure, honey," she said, her voice a little strained. "Your dad wants to talk to you."

"Okay, sure." I heard the phone pass between them.

"Yeah," Dad said, and I cringed. I knew from that one syllable that he was drunk. "What is this crap about a dog?"

I cleared my throat. "Well, I found this dog that I love, and Brad's not too keen on getting one yet, so I thought I could buy it and he'd come around—"

"What? Why would you go against his wishes?" he raised his voice at me.

"Well, like I said, I hope that when I bring the puppy home he understands."

"What kind of dog is it?" He slurred loudly into my ear.

"A puggle," I said softly. This was going downhill fast. "It's a beagle crossed with a pug."

"What?" he asked crossly.

I repeated my words, this time yelling into the mouthpiece.

"You want a mutt?" he yelled. "You're going against what Brad wants for a fucking mutt?"

"It's an adorable dog, Dad. And I've been so sad, I thought a puppy might help." My voice cracked.

"What?" he shouted into the phone.

"Why can't you hear me?" I shouted back, now annoyed and on the verge of tears.

"You don't go against what your boyfriend wants for a fucking mutt," he said cruelly.

"I don't need this from you," I said coldly. "Give the phone back to Mom."

"We're not going to give you money for a mutt . . . not when Brad said no," he continued to mutter, as if I hadn't said anything.

"I don't want to talk to you about this anymore!" I blurted into the receiver. "Put Mom back on now!"

"WHAT?!" he yelled back at me.

I told him repeatedly to put Mom back on the line.

Finally, Mom seemed to have guessed that something was not right, and she took the receiver back from him.

I was crying by this point. "Why is he drunk?" I asked her on a sob. "And why can't he hear me?"

"He's going deaf. We have ordered a hearing aid for him. And I don't have an answer for you about the drinking, Dee," she said quietly.

"He shouldn't be drinking like that, Mom," I said as I wiped away my tears. "I won't talk to him when he's in this condition anymore."

"I understand. Try not to worry, baby," she said soothingly. "I'll mail you the puppy money tomorrow."

"Thanks, Mom," I said between sniffles.

After we hung up, I had a long, good cry in my car. I watched other motorists pass me by as I sobbed uncontrollably on the side of the road. My stomach was knotted to the point that it caused me pain. I could not believe we were back here with Dad again. I knew mere mortals were not going to resolve this issue for him. I hung my head in a desperate prayer.

Please Lord. Not again. It's going to kill him.

Dee and Shel before Shel's prom.

L-R: Shad, Shannon, Shel, Dee.

L-R: Shannon, Shad, Dee, Shel (the last picture of us together).

L-R: Dee, Shel, Grandpa Harold

Brad and Dee

CHAPTER 15:
SAINT SADIE

*I*t was a three-hour trek through rural Wisconsin to pick up my new puggle. Brad was at work, and angry with me, so I traveled alone. I was excited to meet my new pup and determined to make it a good trip. I brought an eclectic collection of music with me. Green hills rolled and dipped by my car window as I sped toward my puppy. I sang along with my CD player, the day bright and sunny.

I had purchased a kennel that could have housed a greyhound. I had plenty of dog toys and a soft blanket. I intended to spoil her rotten. A couple of times I realized my face was wreathed in a grin. I couldn't remember the last time I had been this happy about something.

I stopped for lunch at a roadside diner and ordered a chicken wrap and fries. I noticed that the clientele were mostly farmers, dressed in tattered jeans and overalls, their faces tanned and lined. I was still about a half-hour from the breeder's home. I ate quickly, paid my bill, and, to quote Willie Nelson, was "on the road again."

I left the main highway to turn onto a gravel road that looked like it led to nowhere. The grasses were overgrown, with large, awkward trees, some of them rotted and broken. I squinted and could see a hobby farm at the end of the road. I pulled into the drive and stopped in front of a small house. Once out of the car, I stretched my limbs. The breeder, Sam, came out to meet me. She was a short, round middle-aged woman with sandy hair and glasses.

"Hi, I'm Sam!" she said with a huge smile. "You must be Dee?"

"I am!" I said with a laugh as I took her outstretched hand. "It's nice to meet you."

"Let me take you to your puppy," she said happily, and I turned to follow her.

There were three trailer homes in the yard, and it appeared that they housed the puppies. I could hear dogs barking from all directions. She opened the door to one of the trailers. It occurred to me for a moment that I had walked into a puppy mill, but Sam genuinely seemed to care about the animals. I pushed the idea from my mind.

She showed me Lady, the dam that had produced my pup. She was a stately, older beagle, her teats swollen.

"Her father, Yodel, is around her somewhere," Sam said distractedly.

"No worries," I said, barely able to contain my excitement.

Sam bent over and pointed out my puppy to me. "That's her!" she said with a big smile.

I let out a delighted sigh. "She is adorable!" I said gleefully.

I watched the pup and her brother exchange final kisses, as if they knew of their impending separation. I gently scooped her up and held her in front of my face. I looked into her soft brown eyes and fell in love. She was so small, my hands seemed to engulf her. She gave me kisses and was so excited to meet me.

I chatted with Sam as I nuzzled the puppy and signed paperwork. She gave me a copy of my purchase receipt. Then I tucked my puppy into the ridiculously big kennel and hit the road. We had a fine trip, until the last five miles, when she pooped in the kennel. The world had come to an end, if her yelps were any indication. She needed a bath when we got home. I had to wash the ball Sam had given me, which had the pup's brother's scent on it. It was full of poop, the consistency of diarrhea, so I had no choice.

Thus began our journey together. I named her Sadie, because it was the only name Brad would tolerate. She brought me great joy, but she was also a naughty puppy. She went through her chewing stage, which we combated with dog-deterring bitter apple scent spray. Nevertheless, the legs of our sofa would never be the same. She was quite hard to potty-train and had several accidents that drove us to the brink of our sanity. She had boundless puppy energy and would eat herself to death if we let her. It became apparent that she would need to be on a diet *forever*. Our veterinarian told us she needed to be at 20 lb., and I was determined to keep her at a healthy weight.

I jogged with her and played with her on the living room floor. I scolded her when she was being a terror. It became apparent early on that Brad was the "alpha dog" in the house. I was Sadie's playmate, and Brad was her disciplinarian. I got defiant barks and kisses, and he got respect and kisses. She would even kiss on command.

Sadie was spoiled-rotten and self-important, and she believed that she ruled our home. She was the most intelligent dog I have ever known. She was able to do cost–benefit analysis when she made decisions and was willful to a fault. I fully and readily admit that the poor dog would have been completely ruined if not for Brad. She was too cute for him to be angry at me for too long. He started to train her and taught her all the usual tricks: sit, stay, beg, down, crawl, dance, and roll over. He didn't teach her the speak command, because she did enough of that already. She loved to perform and was full of curiosity. Her nose loved a good adventure.

Contrary to the title of this chapter, Sadie was no saint. The only saintly thing about her was that she saved me. Her sheer naughtiness saved me from my grief over Shel. I couldn't wallow too much because I had to run after her. It was a never-ending chase of stopping this, cleaning that, correcting this, and scolding her.

There were times I would reflect on things and start to cry. She found my tears and the noise I made curious. She would cock her head to one side, then the other, her eyes quizzical. When she couldn't figure me and my emotions out, she would bark at me profusely. This caused me to laugh through my tears and pick her up for a hug. Her barks seemed to say, *why do you do this? What good can come from this thing that you are doing?*

I realized that she was a wise old soul in a puppy's body. "Dog" is "God" spelled backwards, and that cannot be a coincidence. She's not a perfect dog by any means, but she was the perfect dog for my situation. As I look back, she helped me through the worst times of my life.

CHAPTER 16:
THE WEDDING

$\mathcal{S}$ ome friends of ours asked Brad and me to participate in their wedding. After Brad's divorce, he had moved in with Andy for a while. Andy asked out Lana so that we could all double date. We spent a lot of time together during the next few months. Andy had been a bit of a ladies' man before Lana, so it was fun to watch their relationship develop and grow. Andy expressed some doubts to us, but we saw that the relationship was good for him and encouraged him to stay with her. Then, after six months of dating, Lana discovered she was pregnant. Andy's single days were over, but he didn't seem to mind. He asked her to marry him.

This was the catalyst that led Brad to move out, and then we bought our house. Lana had a baby girl they named Kaylee. Her prince had finally come, and Lana planned the wedding of her dreams. Their baby was healthy, and we helped them celebrate each milestone. Brad and I participated in the bachelor and bachelorette parties, respectively. We were fitted for our groomsman tuxedo and bridesmaid dress. There was a flurry of activity to get everything ready in time.

When the big day came, I was almost as giddy as the bride herself. I had to admit, it was wonderful to celebrate something. It seemed like a golden ticket to live joyfully again. Their happiness became my own, and it was long overdue.

Our bridesmaid dresses were sexy—I marveled at my own cleavage. And Brad had never looked more handsome. As is so often the case at weddings, I was reminded of my love for Brad and how lucky I was to have him in my life. I bubbled over with joy and couldn't stop smiling at everyone. I turned my back on my grief for a night and it put a spring in my step.

Andy's mother hosted the ceremony from her backyard. There were beautiful flowers and a fountain. Every detail was perfect. Lana looked so lovely, and Andy was dashing in his tuxedo. It was so easy to get caught up in the loving atmosphere that surrounded them. Andy and Lana came from very different family backgrounds, but everyone got along so splendidly. I really love that about weddings. People that normally wouldn't hang out together suddenly become best friends for a night. The love that emanates from the couple engulfs everyone else, and for a night, it is pure bliss. I teared up a couple of times, I was so glad to be a part of it.

The reception, like all receptions, was where everyone really relaxed and started to party. There were copious amounts of food and booze, and everybody enjoyed themselves immensely. I danced with my love, danced with the bride, dollar-danced with the groom, chicken-danced, bunny-hopped, flirted with bartenders for drink discounts, and wore myself out having a grand time. I requested songs, dragged my feeling-no-pain boyfriend out for dances, and partied with my newfound wedding friends. A picture Lana snapped of Brad and me on the dance floor would tell the story later. He held me tight, my expression soft with love and booze. My face was tipped up toward his and I was on the verge of a laugh. The night went by in a blur, and I loved every minute of it.

I had never thought about marriage all that much. I had told Brad I didn't care if we ever got married. That night started to change my mind. Shel had never known love like I had found with Brad. He would never be able to validate his love on a special day such as this one. It started to matter. It was a wisp of a thought that barely registered with me, but it was as if a seed had been planted.

I was drunk, but still lucid enough to know I shouldn't drive us home. I called a cab for us at nearly 3:00 in the morning. Everyone else had reserved a room for the night, but we lived only fifteen minutes from the reception hall. Our cabbie had no idea where we lived, and he got lost. The ride seemed to last forever, but we finally made it. He cut me a break on the fare and helped me get a stumbling Brad into the house. I closed the door behind him and let out a big sigh. I poured my barely coherent boyfriend into bed. Somehow, I extracted myself from my dress, which was seriously disheveled. I scrubbed off my makeup, popped some Aleve, and drank a massive amount of water. As my head hit the pillow, I shuddered to myself.

This is really going to hurt tomorrow.

Then everything went black.

CHAPTER 17:
THE DROWNING

The next morning my cell phone rang shrilly at half past seven in the morning. I had not made it to bed until almost four, so I let the call roll to voicemail. There was another shrill ring a moment later and I started to come out of my fog. My mind was fuzzy, my eyeballs hurt, and my throat was raw. This caller didn't care about that. They kept calling.

I will give them a piece of my mind. Right after I find my phone. It's here somewhere, dammit!

I found it and saw that it was Carmen.

Oh, no! This is going to be bad.

"Hello?" I answered with a croak.

"Dee?" I heard Carm's voice say. "I'm calling about your dad. He's very sick. He's in the hospital and they don't think he's going to make it."

I snapped to attention, as if someone had backhanded me hard. This call had the power to wrench me out of my alcohol-induced coma.

"What?! Dad is dying?" I asked incredulously, the phone clenched in my hand.

"They think so, yes," she said softly. "Dee, you need to come now."

I squeezed my eyes shut as my mind reeled. "Okay," I heard myself say out loud. "We'll be there as soon as we can."

"Godspeed," Carmen said on a soft sob. "See you soon, love you."

"Love you too. Bye." I hung up and whirled around.

Brad had slept through the call. "Brad," I said sternly. I shook him. It took a couple of attempts before I saw him jerk awake.

"Brad, get up, Dad's dying! We must go to North Dakota, now!" I blurted out.

"What? What's going on?" he mumbled as he sat up in bed. He stared at me through eyes squinted against the overhead light I had switched on.

I didn't stop to explain. I yanked a suitcase out of the closet and threw it on our bed. I started to throw things in it. "I don't know. Carmen just called and told me to come ASAP. It sounds like it will be to say goodbye."

I blinked hard and cleared my throat.

I am not crying right now.

Brad shook his head as if to clear it. I understood his confusion. We didn't have time for the hangovers we so richly deserved. Brad dragged himself to his feet and started to get ready. I discovered my purse was missing; I had forgotten it at the reception hall. My mind whirred as I tried to get a grip and organize my thoughts.

Dad had been in the hospital for a couple of weeks. He had fallen on some ice in a hospital parking lot after a doctor's appointment. His elbow became infected, and he was hospitalized to treat the infection and to have surgery. It had seemed so routine; I hadn't given it much thought.

Now my sister-in-law had called to tell me he was dying. Her words echoed through my mind after I had hung up with her.

You need to come now. Godspeed.

It all sounded bizarre as it bounced around in my brain.

Suddenly I stopped. I had to talk to my brother. I needed to hear it from my own blood.

"Hello?" I heard Shannon say after a couple of rings.

"What is going on with Dad?" I asked shrilly. I clutched my phone in both hands.

"Well, the doctors are worried. He's become septic, but they are hopeful that he will recover," he replied.

I knew what that meant. It wasn't good. "Okay," I said tentatively. "We'll be there in a bit."

"Sounds good. Drive safe; love you," he said.

"Love you, too." I hung up.

I was somewhat reassured after the call, but I didn't slow down. Brad and I finished with our suitcase and got Sadie ready to go. I called the reception hall, explained the situation, and asked them to hold my purse until we returned from our trip. Brad would foot the bill for the trip.

I sighed heavily as my shoulders took on weight that I wasn't ready to bear. If only I could return to the night before. I wanted to have fun and continue my break from reality. The reality I faced now filled me with dread.

Brad turned into a NASCAR driver and got us to Bismarck in record time. A trip that normally takes six and a half hours took us a little over four. I had a story ready for the cops if we got pulled over.

My father is dying, officer. He's dying and I need to get there fast. Either back off or give us an escort to the hospital. No license and registration for you today; stick your speeding ticket where the sun doesn't shine!

Dad was in the ICU at St. Alexius Hospital. On the way to his room, I walked by the room that had been Shel's. That was a mind trip so eerie that I couldn't get a grip on it. I couldn't believe I was there again. Brad shepherded me into Dad's room, and I gasped. Dad was intubated, like Shel had been before his Rochester trip. He breathed with the assistance of a machine. There was no response from him as I entered his room. Eerie didn't begin to explain it. It was downright gut-wrenching for me.

My brothers, Mom, and I took turns at his bedside. Dad was never alone; Mom was almost always with him. Occasionally, she would go to Shad's place to sleep or freshen up. She was holding up well, but I could tell she was scared; we all were. He wasn't responding to treatment. He seemed to be in limbo.

We were alone, and I held Dad's hand. Shel had taught me to never assume recovery was on the way. I knew this was an opportunity I might not get again.

"I'm here, Dad," I said softly as I stroked his hand. "I've come to visit you. Don't worry about anything, okay? We're all here, Dad. We're all here for you."

His eyes were closed. He didn't squeeze my fingers back.

"I forgive you, Dad," I said quietly. "I forgive you for all the bad things you did when you were drinking. I forgive you for the things you did when you weren't yourself. You were always there when I needed you. You've been a great dad to me in all the ways that really mattered. Don't forget that, okay? And please don't worry, Dad. I know you're a Wahl and we like to worry, but please don't. Everything is going to be okay. I love you, Dad. I will always love you."

I continued to stroke his hand. I kissed his face. I watched for a reaction—there was nothing. Just the hiss of the ventilator and the beeps from his heart rate monitor. I was somewhat comforted by the fact that his vitals looked solid.

"Dad!" I said loudly, as I remembered he was going deaf. "Dad, it is Dee. Can you look at me? Can you open your eyes, Dad?"

He did not respond, and I tried not to be frustrated. I knew there was a clock ticking and he had to pull out of this soon.

The doctors had repaired his elbow in surgery, but they were not prepared for his inability to recover. They confirmed that his infection had spread. This had caused him to go into septic shock. The sepsis would lead to organ failure and low blood pressure if they couldn't get it under control. His condition was further complicated by his body going into withdrawal. His return to alcohol over the past few months had caught up with him. He didn't have the immune system needed to fight the infection properly.

They pushed drugs and tried different tactics to revive him, but he failed to respond to any of it. Ultimately, they had done all they could do, and now it was up to him.

On the third day that we were there, Shannon and Carmen called to say they were on their way to the hospital. Brad and I met them there. We all sat with Dad for a while and looked for some sign from him, but none came. Mom had gone to Shad's to rest.

We looked at each other with sad eyes. We made small talk as Dad's ventilator and monitors beeped and whirred.

"Let's go grab a bite to eat and chat," Shannon said finally.

"Sounds good," I said. "Where do you want to go?"

"Ground Round?" It was a nearby restaurant.

"Sure. We'll meet you there," I replied as we gathered our things to leave.

We arrived at Ground Round and found a table. It was somewhat busy, but we could talk easily and hear each other. We ordered our food.

"I can't believe we're at this point with Dad," I said heavily.

"I know. It's not really a surprise, given that he hasn't taken care of himself, but still, I did not think it would happen this soon," Shannon replied.

"I know it. And I'm worried about Mom," I said. "She seems like she's taking everything in stride, but I know this is taking a toll on her."

"Certainly," Shannon said with a furrowed brow. "And what happens if he ends up in a nursing home? The doctors seem to be pushing that, but Mom and Dad have zero savings. A nursing home is going to bleed them dry."

"Yes, it will," I said with a nod of agreement. "But I can't think about that right now. One thing at a time."

Shannon met my gaze across the table. "How do you think he's doing?"

I took a deep breath. I was determined not to pull punches like I had with Shel. It wasn't fair when I knew better. I didn't want to deprive anyone of the chance to say goodbye if it came to it.

"He doesn't look good, Shannon," I said with resignation. "He isn't breathing above the ventilator very much, which is what he needs to do to be extubated. The machine is doing most of the work for him. That's not a good sign. The longer he's on it, the harder it will be to come off it."

"That would be like hell on earth for your dad," Carmen said with conviction. "To have to stay hooked up to machines long-term."

We all murmured our agreement.

"This is so odd," I said thoughtfully after a moment. "It's a weird feeling when you have to start thinking like a parent for your parents."

"Yeah," Shannon acknowledged. "Like I said, I didn't think it would happen this soon."

Eventually, the conversation moved on to other topics. Our minds needed a break from the sorrow and circumstances we faced. We told stories and jokes, especially Shannon and Brad. It was so good to laugh and forget for a moment that our hearts were breaking. I'm glad we took that time together, because the days ahead were dark for us.

CHAPTER 18:
NO MORE SECOND CHANCES

Two days later, we broke away to go to a football game of Cody's. Mom was at the hospital with Dad, so it was just the siblings and their significant others in the stands. I cheered for Cody and his teammates with gusto. The game was a reminder that life still went on outside the hospital. It was an easy thing to forget within the four walls of Dad's stark white hospital room.

After the game, I asked my brothers to meet me in the parking lot to talk about Dad and our options. They agreed and sent their kids off to play at a nearby park.

I mentally gathered my medical knowledge and observations. I squared my shoulders and braced myself. I put my hands on my hips and defied my little-sister image to the best of my ability. Brad stood close behind me; I soaked up his silent, emotional support like a sponge. I took a deep breath and began to speak.

"Dad is doing very poorly, you guys," I began tentatively. "He still isn't breathing above the vent. He isn't responsive and his systems are starting to fail. We need to figure out what to do now."

"What do you mean he isn't breathing above the vent?" Shad asked.

"It means that he hasn't tried to breathe on his own in any meaningful way," I explained. "If he was breathing on his own, they would wean him off the vent, and then pull the breathing tube. Dad is taking very few breaths on his own."

Shad nodded and spat on the ground.

"Well, what you do you think we should do, Dee?" Shannon asked after a moment.

I let out a long breath. "I don't believe we should take any extreme measures to save him," I stated matter-of-factly. "Either he pulls out of this or he doesn't. It's very difficult for me to say that, but he's so weak. If he goes, we should let him go, because that's what Dad would want us to do."

"Are you sure?" Shannon asked. "Do you believe we've done everything we can?"

"I believe we have, yes," I replied softly. "With that said, I don't have a crystal ball. I'm not sure what's going to happen. He might recover next week, or this might go on for months. If that's what happens, then we'll have other decisions to make. The scenario I'm talking about is if he codes. If his heart stops and he quits breathing, do we want him resuscitated? That's the decision I think we should make now."

"I see," Shannon said thoughtfully. "Well, if that were to happen, I think we should let him go. I don't think Dad would want us to take extreme measures, either."

"Shad?" I asked expectantly.

"I agree," he said without preamble.

"Okay, so we're all in agreement," I said quietly. "I appreciate everyone staying to talk about this. It's something that's been on my mind, and I wanted to know how you guys felt about it."

"Of course," Shannon said. "We're all in this together."

"Thanks, Dee," Shad said as his gaze met mine.

We talked a bit more and then parted ways.

When we were both in our car, I turned to Brad. "Well, that's over," I choked as I burst into tears. "That was so hard, Brad."

"I know it was," he said softly as he awkwardly hugged me across the console. "But you did great."

We headed back to his mother's house to retire for the night. My mind drifted to a conversation from the past.

"You know, Dad told me he had to make this decision for his dad," I mused aloud as my tears dried on my cheeks. "Grandpa had suffered a stroke. He lived with it for six years and then started to severely decline. He was eighty-three and barely coherent at the end. It fell to Dad to decide if he would meet his fate sooner rather than later. Dad elected to sign the Do Not Resuscitate (DNR) form. He said that the decision had always haunted him. He basically signed a paper that said it was okay for his father to die. Now, here I am, doing it for him. I just told my brothers that it's okay to let Dad die. I hope this is the right decision."

"You did the right thing," Brad said as he took my hand. "You have to take emotion out of it and think about what he would want if he could decide for himself."

"Yeah. I just feel in my heart that he wouldn't want to live like this," I said softly as I watched a sea of fall colors whiz by my window. "In a past conversation, he said that if something happened to him, he wouldn't want to be on life support. Still, even knowing that, I wouldn't wish this decision on anyone. I feel like I've signed a death warrant for my own father. Even though I know it's the right thing, it's one of the hardest things I've ever had to do."

"Of course, it is," Brad responded as he squeezed my hand, his dark eyes sympathetic. "You're doing the best you can with the information that you have. That's all you can do."

I nodded and fell silent. I stared out my window with eyes that didn't see.

There won't be any more second chances for him.

The thought jolted me in my seat. For every fork in the road of his life, he had chosen alcohol. Now his alcohol addiction was an accomplice to his demise. A non-drinker would likely have beaten this infection. All the warnings he had from doctors and loved ones had been to no avail. Dad had good genes and should have lived a long life. A heart attack, stroke, or cancer—these diseases were beyond human control. Dad had brought this upon himself, which made everything that much harder to bear.

I blinked back tears that burned my tired eyes.

How could you do this to us, Dad?

If he got better, he would likely go back to booze again. If he didn't get better, he would stay on a ventilator in a nursing home for the rest of his days. If he coded, what would the doctors be saving, exactly? A DNR made sense in that situation. There were some things a defibrillator couldn't fix, and I knew it.

I went to visit Dad with Brad and Kathy on the day before we left for the cities.

I stood by my father and stared at him for a moment. His eyes were closed. His breathing tube was still in place. I watched his chest rise and fall with breaths controlled by the ventilator. I needed something from him, and I couldn't leave until I got it.

I jostled his arm. "Dad," I said near his ear, "it's Dee. Can you open your eyes for me?"

No response.

"Dad!" I yelled. I shook him hard by the shoulders. "Dad! Can you hear me? It's Dee. I need you to talk to me!"

I choked back a sob and left the room to collect myself. I was so desperate for a sign that he might recover from his stupor. I feared I wouldn't get my wish. I walked down the hall, my hands on my hips, head hung low.

God, I'm asking you for another miracle. Please.

Kathy rushed up to me. "Dee, he's awake!"

I ran back to the room and to Brad's side. Dad's eyes had drifted closed again.

"I talked to him," Brad said quietly. "I told him you're here."

"Dad?" I tried. I grabbed his wrist. "Dad, it's Dee. Can you talk to me?"

No response. I bit my lip hard in frustration.

"Dennis!" Brad bellowed loudly, his voice like a thunderclap.

Dad's eyelids flickered open. His beautiful hazel eyes, the eyes he had given to Shel, looked straight into mine. They were bloodshot and glazed over from the drugs, but they were open.

I squeezed his hand so hard. "I'm here, Dad. I'm here for you. I came all this way for you to open your eyes like this. Thank God."

He continued to stare into my eyes, and I wondered if he was really there. He did not squeeze my hand back. "I love you, Dad," I told him. "It's going to be okay."

After a few moments his eyes closed, and I sat in a chair by his bed. He needed to rest. For the first time in days, I had hope that things might turn around for him.

The following day was a Sunday, and Brad and I got ready to go home. It was hard for me to leave while Dad's condition was in flux. Brad reasoned that his current condition could continue for several weeks or months; we couldn't continue to miss work. I knew he was right, but that didn't make it easier to go. I was overwhelmed with guilt. I was scared that he would die, and I wouldn't be there. I worried that he would call for me and I would be gone.

We picked up my purse on the way home and I returned to work the next day. My schedule showed I was off on Tuesday. I was grateful, because I wanted some time to recover from the trip. I needed to catch my breath.

God, grant me the serenity to accept the things I cannot change, cour-age to change the things I can, and wisdom to know the difference

. —Reinhold Niebuhr

CHAPTER 19:
A BROKEN HEART

*T*he next day, September 19, 2006, it rained hard all day. In the afternoon, I sat on the sofa while I folded laundry. Brad and I chatted while we watched TV. I was almost cheerful. Mom had called me that morning to tell me the hospital staff had removed Dad from the ventilator the night before. That had to be a good sign.

Maybe, just maybe, Dad would beat the odds again.

My cell phone rang shrilly and interrupted our conversation. The caller ID said it was Shannon.

"It's Shannon," I told Brad as I muted the TV.

"Hello?" I answered the phone with a smile.

"Dee, I have something to tell you," He began softly. "Dad died fifteen minutes ago."

"What?" I screeched. A sob tore through me. "What happened? I thought he was doing better?"

"I don't know," Shannon said. "Mom just called to tell me and she's hysterical. I wanted you to be prepared."

In the next moment, I was hysterical. I could barely breathe between hard sobs. I had explained to my family that this could happen, but until that moment, I believed in my dad. He was supposed to prove me wrong.

All at once, it hit me like a ton of bricks that I had lost my father. One of the two people that had given me life had been taken from me. It seemed like I had lost Shel yesterday and now Dad was gone.

I cried into the phone. My lungs heaved painfully within my chest. It was several moments before I was able to converse with Shannon.

No hope. No miracles. Just empty holes where Shel and Dad used to be.

I took a deep, quavering breath. "I'm sorry," I choked out. "I just can't believe he's gone."

"I know," Shannon said sadly. "Mom's really taking it hard. I guess Aunt Lettie came to see him. Mom arrived and Aunt Lettie left shortly after. Dad died about fifteen minutes after she left. Mom was alone with him when it happened."

"I see," I said quietly. "Did she just call you?

"Yes. Try to get it together before you talk to her, okay?"

"Okay," I responded. A beep sounded in my ear. I looked at my cell display and saw Mom's name. "She's calling now, Shan. I'll talk to you later."

"Alright. Take care; talk soon."

I switched over to Mom's call. "Hello?" I said hesitantly.

"Dee?" I heard Mom say. "It's Mom. Honey, I'm sorry to tell you this, but your dad just passed away."

She had saved the hysterics for Shannon, because her voice sounded calm to me. She had collected herself before she called me.

"I know, Mom," I said gently. "Shannon just called to tell me. I'm so sorry. I thought he was doing better. Why did they take him off the vent?"

"They wanted to see how your dad would do without it," Mom said on a trembling breath. "He went downhill fast after that. He could breathe on his own, but his stomach was rejecting the food from his feeding tube. The food was literally not moving through his system at all. They did everything they could for him, but his organs failed him."

"Did he know what was going on?" I asked, desperate for anything she could tell me about his final moments.

"I think so. He couldn't talk. He looked at me with pleading in his eyes and it about broke my heart. He was trying so hard, but nothing would work for him. I started to pray over him. I asked Jesus to please come and take him. I saw a moment of panic on his face as I prayed, and then there was peace. He was just gone."

Tears streamed down my face. "I'm so sorry you were alone, Mom."

"It's okay, baby," she said softly. I knew she was crying, too. "Dad is with Jesus now."

"I hope so, Mom. Brad and I will be back as soon as we can."

"Okay, honey. We'll see you then," she said, and we hung up.

I was thirty-one years old. Shel and Dad were gone, and we were down to four. Four of us left. This was my third family funeral in less than a year.

By that point, I hated that gray suit of mine. That thing was bad luck. I wanted to buy something new. Dad had worn a green suit to Shel's funeral. I decided my pantsuit would be green for Dad's funeral.

Two days! Why the hell didn't I stay two more days?

My last time at his bedside was the last time I saw him alive. His hazel eyes had locked with mine for a few moments.

Did he even know I was there?

Brad heard my side of the conversation. I stood up on wobbly legs. He came to hold me without words. Fresh tears sprang to my eyes.

Here we go again.

We packed our belongings side by side and prepared to make the long trip back.

CHAPTER 20:
DAD AND SHEL

*D*ad and Shel had a complex relationship. They were very different people. Dad was all bluster and fire, while Shel was calm, cool water. Dad liked to yell and speak his mind and Shel was quiet and introspective. Dad made waves, while Shel liked to go with the flow. There wasn't much common ground between them.

Certain things about their relationship baffle me to this day. For one, Dad never taught Shel how to fight. He took Shannon and Shad down into the basement for fighting lessons. He taught them how to take punches and give punches and how to protect themselves. Shel did not receive any such lesson from him. There were a couple of times in his life it would have been good if he'd known how to defend himself. He ended up on the hurting end of some bad fights.

Did Dad think Shel wasn't the fighting type, so he didn't teach him?

Shel didn't appreciate Dad's tendency toward violence in situations, either. We went to visit my Grandma Jane in Las Vegas, and Shel had taken off on her 10-speed. He was gone for hours. I was almost eighteen at the time, so Shel was fifteen. My parents feared the worst as it grew dark, and Shel was nowhere to be found. We called for him, walked the neighborhoods, but there was no Shel.

Dad's fears manifested into anger. When we found Shel a few blocks over, Dad was out of the car in an instant. He struck Shel in the face for the worry he had caused him.

"Where the fuck have you been? We've been looking everywhere for you! Don't you ever go off like this again, dammit!" He raged at him in the middle of the street.

I will never forget the look on Shel's face—baleful, shocked, and full of sadness. I saw blatant hatred on his face, and it startled me. He seemed like he wanted to hit Dad back, but he didn't. Instead, he bowed his head and didn't say a word. We got into the car and headed back to Grandma Jane's. Dad berated him the entire car ride.

Mom and Dad treated Shel differently after his accident—they were more protective of him than of the rest of us. As the only girl, I was the recipient of some of that, too. It was as if Shel and I were raised differently than our older brothers. Shel seemed to resent that a little bit. He wanted to be treated the same as his brothers, but his relationship with our parents had a different dynamic, and he knew it. Not only had they almost lost him once but he also had medical conditions that required him to stay with them. He also didn't want to leave Mom to fend off Dad alone.

He once told Shannon as tears streamed down his face, "I don't feel like I can leave her behind. I'm the only one left to protect her. How can I leave her to face him alone? What will happen if I'm not there?"

Two months before he died, he had said to Mom, "I don't think I'm ever going to make it out of Tuttle."

"Of course, you will, Shel," she reassured him. "In a couple of months, your birthday will be here, and you'll have your money. You'll get your license back and we'll get you a car. You can move into your own place."

Shel nodded and said nothing further about it. He walked away.

When Mom told me that story, it was like an ice bath to my soul. Somehow, he knew those things would not come to pass. He was a caged bird. Two months must have seemed like an eternity. I knew the things that must have gone through his mind:

Can I get my license back?

Will Dad let me go or interfere?

Will the money really be mine?

Can I live with myself if something happens to Mom after I leave?

It turned out he was right; Shel never got to spread his wings and fly away. He didn't get a chance to work things out with Dad. So many things were left unsaid between them. Dad's regret as he peered into Shel's coffin spoke volumes.

There were times when light was not refracted but allowed to shine through. When Shel was at Medcenter, a multitude of tests were ordered as they tried to determine the cause of his headache. The decision was made to do a spinal tap. Shel asked Dad to stay with him through it. He didn't ask for his mother; he asked for his dad. The memory of that request always made Dad cry.

In high school, a girl had ditched Shel during a date in Bismarck. She jumped out of his car at a stoplight and jumped in with her friends. Shel called Dad and asked him to talk to him as he drove home.

Dad leaned heavily on Shel when Mom ended up in the hospital. When Dad was at a loss, his youngest son stepped in to lighten his load. Shel would sit in the backseat with Mom and keep her calm while Dad drove them to the hospital.

I know Shel wanted Dad to be proud of him. At the end of the day, a son wants his father's approval. There were intricacies to their relationship that I'll never know or understand. It's a puzzle that is missing some of the pieces.

When I found out that Dad died, my first prayer was a fervent hope that Shel had gone to greet him. For all their differences in this life, I prayed that the next one held forgiveness and peace.

CHAPTER 21:
DAD AND ME

*D*ad was very flawed. He never would have won the father of the year award, not even close. He was a domineering, strong-willed man with a hot temper and a sharp tongue that could cut me to the bone. It was hard to write his obituary. I wanted to say good things about him, but I was mad at him. He had left me when I still needed my father. He had never chosen our family first. It had always been about booze for him.

My Aunt Lettie once told me regretfully, "He was such a happy-go-lucky kid. Tender-hearted and kinder than his sisters. I'm so sorry you never got to truly know him. He started drinking in high school, so even your mother did not know him without alcohol."

He had beaten his illness for a time, but the loss of Shel sent him right back to it. I hated his weakness. I hated that he hadn't been strong enough to choose life over his grief.

Be strong and speak your mind.

Be true to your word.

You're a Wahl—act like it.

What good were any of his mantras when he hadn't lived up to them himself?

Shel's death had stolen Dad from me. Dad's heart had been broken and now his body had followed. There were so many things that would never be made right. I was full of rage and bitter tears that never seemed to end. I wanted to claw through the wedge that was now between us.

Why did death have to win again?

My burning anger was eventually replaced with the dull ache of deep sorrow and some regret. I want to talk about what has been lost. Dennis Wahl wasn't a good person in many ways. Our relationship was very complicated, but he was still my father. I loved him, and the reasons why are hard to fit in an obituary.

When I was a little girl, he voiced his chagrin to my mother, "I don't know what to do with her. Boys, I know—but what do I do with *her*?"

This surprised me, because Dad and I had been close. He had figured out how to relate to me somewhere along the way.

Mom told me, "Your dad would talk to the boys about life decisions and the news headlines. With you, he was different."

When I was a child, he would talk to me about music, movies, and books.

He told Mom once, "She's my most level-headed child, and I'm proud of the person she's become."

We had this great father–daughter rapport, especially during his sober times. For a total of three years, I knew my dad as a sober man, and it was wonderful.

We would talk for hours on the phone. He would say, "Well, I guess we should go . . .," and then he'd think of something and the call would go for another hour.

Dad was a highly intelligent man and a born storyteller. I got glimpses of the tender-hearted Dennis that Aunt Lettie told me about. He would tell me a story and his breath would catch in his throat. Sometimes he would cry. It was a side of him that he strove to keep from the boys, but he didn't mind sharing it with me.

Dad told me the same stories repeatedly. His favorites were from when he had dated and married Mom in Las Vegas. He loved basketball, pickled herring, and pig's feet. He had played trombone in high school, and he preferred Cadillacs. Dad loved to read. He would tell me his book wish list, and I would have them for him by his next birthday or for Christmas.

I bought him CDs and made mixed tapes of his favorite music. As a little girl, I would sit with him on Sunday evenings, just the two of us. We listened to Sinatra or Dean Martin, and he would reminisce about Las Vegas and his youth. Sinatra was his favorite singer, and he loved the song *My Way*. That song was an anthem for him and how he had lived his life.

Dad had been a very handsome man. Classmates had told him he looked like Gene Kelly in his graduation picture. His years of hard living and drinking had taken their toll, but when I gazed at him in his casket, he looked young to me. Dad was sixty-six when he died.

My favorite picture of him was taken right before my junior prom. He had his glasses on, his hair a little askew. He smiled at my mother, who was behind the camera. I had hugged him, my lips puckered in a kiss on his cheek. I had kicked up my leg behind me in that old Hollywood style, decked out in full prom-dress glory. We were mid-laugh, hamming it up for the camera.

I loved his twinkling hazel eyes and his smile. He didn't make a sound when he laughed. His body would shake, his laugh inward, a loud snort escaping him at the end. He was fiercely protective of me and stood up for me whenever I needed him. I had dreamed of him walking me down the aisle at my wedding one day.

His intelligence, his humor, his hands, his voice—these are the things I try to pull back to memory. I try not to let his flaws define him as my father. I want to remember him as he would want me to remember him. I cling to the hours-long phone calls, the hugs we shared, the kisses good-night. These are the things that made him my dad. As for the rest, it is not my place or right to judge how he lived his life.

However, I did have collateral damage left over from his actions. The weight of my anger and disappointment in him crushed me. It compounded my grief and made me a giant ball of resentment. I had to figure out how to forgive him, or I would go mad with it. I could not change what he had done, so I had to change me.

I was a jagged stone and time was like a trickling brook that flowed over me. I visited the same places in my mind, and time smoothed my rough edges and provided clarity. It made me realize that my forgiveness was never meant for my father. It was for me. It did not make what he did okay. Forgiveness was about moving forward for me. It was acceptance. I would not let his past transgressions define him for me. I chose to remember the good. The rest I classified as lessons. Some lessons were for him, and some were for me. Forgiveness is not something I did and then forgot. I had to forgive him repeatedly. Sometimes it took formidable effort to climb that mountain, but when I did, I always found more peace at the top.

For better or worse . . . I am my father's daughter.

CHAPTER 22:
CHOICES

Mom was not there when we planned Dad's funeral. As with Shel, I did not understand her decision, but I had to respect her wishes, nonetheless. Dad's remaining three children gathered around the familiar oval table at the funeral home. We powered through the planning of our father's funeral together.

My brothers had brought their wives, and this time around, I had Brad with me. His presence added something sorely needed, which was an impartial opinion, as well as an excuse to make light of things. In such a dire situation, it was almost pleasant to have someone there to entertain. Before the funeral attendant came to act as mediator, we cracked jokes, mostly at Brad's expense, which he accepted with graceful humor.

When we fell silent, Brad said, "Listen, I'd prefer if I wasn't mentioned in Dennis' obituary."

I already knew the reason—at least the one he had given me at the time—but everyone else in the room was visibly intrigued.

"Why wouldn't you want to be in the obit?" Carmen asked him curiously.

"Yeah, what gives, Brad?" Shannon asked right behind her.

"Well . . ." Brad said on a deep breath. "On Shel's obit, I was listed as Dee's *special friend*, and it made me feel like a freak! Boyfriend sounds too juvenile. We're not engaged, so I'm not her fiancé. We're in fact shacking up, and there's just not a good way to put that on paper. So *special friend* was used for lack of a proper phrase to describe our relationship."

Everyone nodded in agreement, but Brad wasn't finished.

"Really? *Special friend*? Should I just put on a helmet and ride the short bus now?" He said in a heavy-tongued voice tinged with a lisp.

"Ah, poor Brad, the special friend!" Shannon howled as we all laughed hard enough for tears to roll down our cheeks.

We were so loud, the staff at the funeral home probably thought we were crazy, but I didn't care. I soaked in everyone's laughter. I took a mental snapshot of my loved ones' smiling faces and tucked them away in my mind. In the months to come, when things got hard, I shuffled through a small rolodex of stolen, precious moments.

We had to bite back our laughter and hastily compose ourselves when the doorknob started to rattle under the funeral attendant's hand. We shared one last secret glance of glee before we got down to business.

Dad wanted to be cremated. Because of this, we rented a casket for his wake and chose a small wooden one for his ashes, which would be buried later. The songs were chosen by Liz and me earlier. She was going to sing at Dad's funeral, just as she had at Shel's. I had chosen "How Great Thou Art." Dad and I had discussed the hymn in the past. We both agreed it would be a good choice for a funeral song. The other song choice came from Liz and Aunt Lettie—a stirring ballad called "The Anchor Holds." It was as if it had been written with my father in mind—the lyrics were so evocative of his life struggle.

We chose a program with a lovely poem about Dad going home to meet his heavenly Father. The reverend was someone that had known my father. The pianist was the daughter of Dad's classmate. Every detail seemed perfect. I was disappointed with so many aspects of Shel's funeral, but we had done right by Dad. It was important to me to pay attention to the smallest of details this time around. I would regret a great many things as I grieved, but how we planned Dad's funeral was not one of them.

Brad's story resulted in my family calling him my special friend for months. He laughed it off and told me, "It was all worth it. You guys needed to laugh that day. I'm glad I could provide a moment's relief from everything."

Brad eventually told me the real reason he didn't want to be in the obituary. "I knew your dad wanted us to be married. He never said it, but I knew it and I let him down. I didn't want to be mentioned on his obit because I didn't give him what he wanted."

CHAPTER 23:
STORMY WEATHER

I stayed with Brad and Kathy during Dad's wake, funeral, and burial. I should have been with my mother, but again, the house in Tuttle held so many memories. When Mom said she was fine, I told myself I believed it, but I knew better. If that house haunted me, it surely haunted her too. My heart breaks as I imagine how quiet it must have been in that house. I failed her, but I was barely hanging on to my own wits. Brad and Kathy helped assuage my pain. I extended an invitation to Mom to come and stay with us, but she declined. Perhaps her feelings were the opposite of mine, and the house was a comfort to her. I didn't know and I didn't ask. I kept everything close to me emotionally because I was so afraid that I would fall apart.

I dressed in my dark green suit and applied makeup like a robot. I had an odd sense that I wanted to retain some sort of normalcy. I found it ridiculous even as I complied. I was a complete wreck, and for a moment I wanted to show up looking like one. Instead, I did my normal routine—foundation to cover up my red nose, mascara on lashes that would be wet with tears, blush on my pale cheeks. Maybe there is comfort in these futile gestures; maybe going through the motions helps.

I was numb as I walked out to the car. I checked to make sure my purse was full of tissues. Brad drove and Kathy took the back seat. We stopped at Wendy's before we left for Tuttle. As was often the case when I was upset, I didn't realize how hungry I was until I started to eat. We finished our meal and made the solemn hour-long drive. We drove straight to the Methodist Church; the same place Shel's funeral had been. I was curious to see how many people would show up, since Dad had made his fair share of enemies. It was a pleasant surprise to see that many people had come to pay their respects.

How many are here to make sure he's dead?

Dad had lived in Tuttle most of his life and must have seemed like a permanent fixture there. He was the go-to guy for information regarding Tuttle's past or people. I saw many sad faces. Some I didn't know, and I wondered how they had known my father. I should have asked, visited with them, and thanked them for coming. Instead, I gravitated toward the people that I knew.

The same aunts, uncles, cousins, nieces, and nephews that showed up for Shel's funeral were back again, and it was such a comfort. I was glad to see Aunt Lettie, because more than ever, she was a link to my father. As I had expected, I liked Dad's service much more than Shel's. Since Reverend Pozgay had known my father, the service was more poignant and heartfelt. That would be my best advice when a loved one is lost. Someone that knew them should officiate or speak at the service. Those personal touches honored my father and made all the difference. Dad would have approved.

A sweet moment came when I stepped out into the churchyard for a breath of fresh air. Mom's new chihuahua puppy ran through the yard with Spook, a miniature schnauzer I would always think of as Shel's dog. She had named the new puppy Jett, and his pure happiness at being outside in the sun made me smile. He had that clumsy puppy gait and he and Spook chased each other.

I bent and scooped Jett into my cupped hands. His puppy breath and tongue were on my cheek. The world came into focus again for a few moments. Most of what I remember is a whirlwind. Dad in a casket. A good-bye kiss on his forehead. Familiar faces and warm hugs. Coffee and cookies and stories. Whispers goodbye. That moment with Jett was the greatest of them all. I could almost hear Dad's voice in my ear as I held him.

You're going to be okay, Dee.

The last stragglers left the church. We stood together as a family in the church foyer. I hugged Mom first, then my brothers and their wives. I embraced each of my nieces and nephews. There was nothing left to do but leave, so we did.

Once in the car, I started to cry. Brad and Kathy soothed me and soon my tears eased. We stopped for dinner at Peacock Alley Bar and Grill in Bismarck. I ordered some comfort food and treated myself to chocolate mud pie dessert.

If I keep eating like this, I'm going to weigh 300 lb.

"I can't believe Dad is gone," I said aloud to the table.

"I think losing Shel was more than he could bear," Brad said quietly.

"Your family has been through a rough last year, that's for sure," Kathy responded.

"I feel bad leaving Mom like that," I said softly.

"I'm sure she understands," Brad replied, covering my hand with his.

I am a coward.

Kathy changed the subject, and we made small talk as we finished our pie. Afterward, we went back to Kathy's. I changed into comfortable clothes and snuggled with Sadie on the couch. We watched a movie.

My mind wandered. It was odd to be without a father.

I had him longer than a lot of kids have their dads.

My feeble attempts at consoling myself fell flat. I petted Sadie absently. I had no idea how I would bear everything that had happened. I only knew I needed to find a way.

A couple of days later we buried Dad. He had made it clear that he wanted to be cremated. Unfortunately, the crematory nearest to Tuttle was out of commission. His body had to be shipped to Fargo for cremation and then back to Tuttle. When it arrived, we trekked out to Tuttle's cemetery to bury the small coffin that contained our father's remains.

There was no attendant to help, so Shannon had to dig the hole at the cemetery. I watched him with a sense of awe as he did so. The physical and emotional strength he had to exert to dig up the dirt and then bury him was beyond any that I possessed. Dad's young grandsons used their bare hands to help.

Only a small crew had gathered to lay him to rest: Mom, Shad and Shannon and their families, Brad, Aunt Lettie, and me. Dad would have been pleased that Aunt Lettie showed up. In a way, it seemed appropriate that only a few of us were there, and yet, I was sad that it was just us. The dismal day matched my mood. It was overcast, cold, and drizzling rain. I stood there, my mind wandering brokenly, and then Cody came over to me. He threw his arms around me and buried his head against me. He shook with his sobs. His anguish cut me to my core.

Poor Cody. Lord, please help him.

Cody had been Dad's pet, and without a doubt, his favorite grandchild. Dad didn't mean to be cruel about it. He saw so much of himself in Cody that he couldn't help it. My tears renewed as it hit me. Their relationship had been stolen from Cody at the age of fourteen, right when he needed Dad the most.

"Your grandpa loved you so much. He was so incredibly proud of you. Don't ever forget that," I whispered into his ear as I held him tight.

Cody tightened his grip and then broke away. He stared into the grave. The naked loss and pain written across his face clawed at my heart.

After it was over, I hugged Aunt Lettie. "Thank you for being here," I said as I met her gaze.

"I wouldn't miss it. It's good to see you, kid," she said softly.

She carried pieces of Dad with her, and it comforted me like few other things did. I liked to think that Dad saw things through her. After Shel died, he came to me through nature. He whispered to me from the trees, I saw him in the clouds, or felt him on a breeze. This time, though, was different.

I had imagined Aunt Lettie as my parent in the past, when things were rough in my childhood. I had daydreamed of a life without a drinking parent. My visits to Liz's house as a child gave me glimpses into a normal life. Now, as we buried my father, I could almost see him standing next to Aunt Lettie. His eyes were sad that he hadn't followed a path closer to hers. I imagined that he realized now, in death, that he should have chosen his family all along.

After the burial, Aunt Lettie declined our offer to join us and drove home. We headed back to Mom's house. We had a snack while we sat and talked about Dad. The conversation turned and then something happened that shocked me. The boys decided to divide up Dad's guns. I sat there awestruck as they chattered and handed guns to each other.

They are like vultures. We buried Dad like an hour ago.

Something seemed odd and cold about it, but I decided not to judge them over it. Maybe in some weird way it was a comfort to them to take home their father's guns. I had no interest in the guns myself, but it made me think about what I treasured from my relationship with Dad.

What means something to me? What can I take home?

Music. Our shared love of music. I decided to take home some of the CDs I had bought for Dad. I grabbed a few, most of them by Sinatra.

"What are you doing?" I heard Shad ask from behind me.

I turned around and said, "I wanted to take some of Dad's CDs home with me."

"You should leave them for now," he said harshly. "Mom doesn't need to see you taking anything right now."

Oh, but it's okay for you to take his guns home?

I swallowed hard. "I bought them for him, and I don't see the harm in taking them."

"You hardly ever come home, Dee. You don't have the right to take them," he said coldly.

He might as well have slapped me. The irony of our exchange would have struck me as funny if I hadn't been so angry.

Who are you to say this to me? You fucking hypocrite. I know exactly how much you call our parents and how often you go to see them.

My stomach was raw and twisted painfully. My face burned and must have been lobster red. Anger seemed to lick each one of my nerve endings. I was about to heatedly defend myself, but with herculean effort, I refrained.

I am not going to get in a fight with him when we just buried Dad. Not today.

I closed my eyes for a moment, took a deep breath, and sighed it out. "I'm taking them, Shad. I'm sorry if you don't understand why."

He wisely said nothing and walked away. I sent up a quick prayer of gratitude. The idea of a showdown at that moment was a double dose of my worst nightmare.

The gravity of our loss hit me at that moment. Dad had been the glue. The hard-nosed, loud-mouthed obey-or-else peacekeeper of our family. We would never be the same again.

Don't let us fall apart, Lord. Remind us to love one another.

It was a prayer I would pray many times in the days to come. The loss of our father was like someone had pulled an integral piece of wood from our family Jenga. There would always be permanent fractures in our family structure going forward. No one could fix what had broken, and I mourned the death of the family I had known.

CHAPTER 24:
A DAUGHTER'S BLAME

*I*t was not long before I began to blame my mother for my father's death. Slowly the story began to seep out of Mom, and the tidbits she divulged filled me with dismay.

"Your dad was having trouble with the TV remote. He couldn't figure it out," she told me one afternoon.

On a different phone call, she said, "Your dad had a hard time buttoning his shirt near the end. He also complained about his memory. He said he couldn't remember things like he used to."

"He would eat half a sandwich and then say he was too full. He didn't have much of an appetite at all," she told me on another occasion.

I would frown when she told me these things. Her admissions were obvious warning signs. I couldn't believe she had ignored them and not told us about them. It didn't do any good to tell me after it was too late to help him.

I had seen some warning signs when Mom and Dad stayed with us at Christmas. As I mentioned before, Dad had missed the toilet bowl when he urinated. This was brought to my attention by Brad, who had cleaned up after him a few times. At the time I shrugged it off, but when Mom mentioned these other signs of his distress, I realized it was one symptom of many.

Quite frankly, I despised her for not taking better care of him.

"Why didn't you take him to the hospital, Mom?" I asked her during one of our phone calls.

"We did go," she responded. "The doctors didn't listen. I don't know if it was because he was a drinker or what, but they ignored me. I think because we had been in a few times, they didn't trust your dad to stick to any kind of program."

You should've made the doctors listen, dammit!

"Why didn't you tell us kids about it?" I asked. I tried to speak evenly.

"I didn't want to worry you," she said softly. "I didn't think there was anything you could do."

How dare you! How could you not tell us? We could have saved him!

At first, I kept my thoughts to myself. I said the right things to her, even though I seethed with resentment on the inside. Until one day I completely lost it.

"Why didn't you take better care of him, Mom? You had all these warning signs that you ignored! And if you couldn't help him, why didn't you tell me? I knew people at the hospital. I could have helped him!" I cried out one day, my composure completely gone.

"I don't know what I could have done, Dee. I couldn't put him in West Central again. He never forgave me for doing it before. I tried to talk to the doctors, but they wouldn't listen. I didn't know what else to do," she said quietly.

"I could've helped him, Mom," I said bitterly.

"I'm sorry, baby," she said into the receiver, and the hurt in her voice slashed me.

I started to cry. "I'm sorry, Mom, I have to go."

I hung up on her and we didn't talk again for a while.

As time passed, I realized it wasn't really Mom's fault. She was his wife for thirty-eight years. She had grown tired. He had berated, belittled, and threatened her throughout their marriage. In the end, she gave up on him because he had given up on himself. Deep down where it counts, Dad did not want to be saved.

After Shel died, Dad died with him, but on an eleven-month delay. It started in those last moments he spent with Shel in that stark white room. The incessant beeping from the machines rang in his ears, even as his son lay brain-dead. An hourglass was flipped, and the sands of his life slowly ebbed away. The rest of us, the people that loved him and still needed him here, didn't stand a chance.

I blamed Mom for sins she had not committed. She had been brain-washed by my father. He did what he had to do to feed his addiction. He could be very cruel. He went back to his old ways after Shel died. I didn't have to live with him like she did. I was only hearing snippets of their life together. I didn't truly know what she had endured daily, especially at the end.

There was no doubt in my mind that Dad knew he had failed Shel. Dad would never be able to tell him he was sorry. Time had not afforded them the chance to mend their relationship. They wouldn't come to a mutual understanding when Shel got older. Dad was like a failed astronaut, unable to complete his only mission. He was stranded on the moon alone and it killed him.

On some level, Mom knew there was nothing she could do. We had all tried. He never forgave her for putting him in West Central the first time. She could not go through it all again. Instead of tossing out the life preserver for one last save, she let her love drift out to sea and trusted in fate to make the decision for her.

It took me a while to forgive her. I resented her resignation and weakness.

Then one day, out of the blue, everything came into focus for me. Dad had signed his own death warrant because he didn't take care of himself. Mom had done the best she could do. She wasn't his savior. When Dad died, I wanted to place blame on someone. I wanted to make sense of this great loss in my life.

Even if my mother had been the most diligent of wives, she couldn't have saved him from the fate he chose for himself. Dad had sealed his fate from the moment he'd taken his first drink at fifteen and had liked it a little too much. He had a weakness, an illness, and he chose it over his family and his health. Shel's death was the final straw that broke the camel's back.

I am saved from telling people that my father died of alcoholism. I tell them that he got an infection and died of sepsis. The truth is that he could have beaten death if he'd been healthier of mind and body. Perhaps my mother failed him in some ways, but she didn't cause his death. I am sorry to admit that it took me a while to figure that out.

Once I forgave her, I didn't keep it to myself.

"I have something to tell you, Mom," I said one day during one of our calls.

"What's that, honey?" she responded.

"I blamed you for Dad's death," I said quietly. "I thought there was more that you should have done. I was angry at you for a long time about it."

She stammered into the phone. "Well, Dee, I tried—"

"Mom, stop, let me finish," I interrupted with a sigh. "I know now that it wasn't your fault. If he didn't want help—and he didn't—there's no way to save someone like that. I was blaming you for something you couldn't change. I was hurt and angry and I wanted to blame someone, and it was you. But I was wrong. I just wanted to tell you I'm sorry for that."

She was silent for a moment. "It's okay, baby," she said at last. "I know how hard it is to lose a parent. I'm sorry you're going through this so early in your life. Your dad should have been around for a few more years, so I know it's hard. But I'm still here and I love you. If you ever need anything, just let me know."

"Thanks, Mom," I said softly. "I love you, too."

We hung up and I sat in silence for a few moments. It was as if a weight had been lifted. Once I forgave her, and heard her say that it was fine, I was at peace. I laid the blame to rest at last.

CHAPTER 25:
WRECKED

*M*y grandmother Lois did not attend my father's funeral. She was so bereaved over the death of her son that she couldn't bear to make the trip to Tuttle. It was also like Grandma to not want to be a burden during an already burdensome time. Aunt Lettie arranged for a friend to stay with Grandma while we were gone. I was so grateful to learn of that information later. It didn't occur to me to think about Grandma being left alone. I was too wrapped up in my own grief.

A few days after the funeral, Brad and I went to see Grandma. I will never forget the way she looked when I walked through the door—she looked every bit of her ninety years, and then some.

She looks wrecked.

Her silver-gray hair was unkempt and wayward, which was very unlike her. I saw a depth of sadness in her eyes that mirrored the sadness in my soul. It was all I could do to not throw myself at her feet and weep. I had never seen her look so low in my entire life, and Grandma and I had done a lot of living together. I steeled myself for our conversation. The person that linked us together was gone, and it was so heart-wrenching for both of us.

We started with small talk. Once that was out of the way, it was just the two of us, as if Brad was not in the room.

"I cannot believe everything that has happened," she said slowly, with a sad smile. "First Shel and now your dad. I can't believe they're both gone."

"I know. It doesn't seem real. Sometimes I think they're a phone call away, and then I realize they're not and it just kills me," I said as I shook my head in disbelief.

"I'm so tired," Grandma said in a dull tone. "I'm so tired and unbearably sad. I wish the Lord would just come and take me."

There was resignation behind her words, and I flew into a panic inside.

"You can't go," I said as I looked her square in the eye. "Don't go, Grandma, I can't bear it. I cannot bear to lose you, too. You must be strong. You must hold on for me. Please, Grandma."

Her gaze dropped away from mine, and she shook her head.

The room was in a spin. I could not be a comfort to her in that moment. I had prepared myself for her death for years, but that was all swept away now. All that she was to me flashed through my mind and it made me cling to her like a leech. I begged my ninety-year-old grandmother to stay in this life for me.

What can I say? I can't promise things will get better. I have nothing. Nothing I can say that will make her want to stay here with me.

She looked at me with resolute hazel eyes—our family's trademark hue—and pursed her lips. I realized that she was not going to make any promises to me. We came to a draw.

Keep her here with me, Lord. I need more time. I need more time before I lose her, too.

Our conversation dwindled and Brad and I rose to leave. I leaned into Grandma's recliner and hugged her tightly.

"I love you, Grandma," I whispered. "I'll talk to you again soon."

"I love you, Dee," she responded with a kiss on my cheek. "It was so good to see you again, Brad."

"It's good to see you too, Lois. I wish it was under better circumstances," Brad replied as he leaned in for a quick hug.

After we left, I was haunted by the sight of Grandma in her chair. Her hollow eyes. Her decided resignation and depleted demeanor. She was not the grandma I knew. I was chilled to the bone and numb at the same time. I wanted to comfort her, but I didn't know how. I couldn't make things easier for her.

I can barely take care of myself these days.

I returned to see Grandma with my mother a few days later. She looked better. Her hair was smooth, and she made pleasant small talk. She did not mention our previous conversation. I studied her and it suddenly hit me.

Grandma's being strong for my newly widowed mother. Grandma always puts other people first.

It also might have helped to have a couple of days to collect herself. She had tremendous faith, and I knew Jesus could comfort her like no one else.

Grandma was just tired the other day. She's going to be fine.

I believed what I needed to believe.

CHAPTER 26:
PRETENDING

B rad and I went back to the cities. I rested at home for a couple of days, and then went back to work. Once again, the hospital staff, especially the nurses, were wonderful to me. They responded with unfailing sympathy and tenderness. Just as with Shel, I told Dad's story repeatedly, and it was like therapy for me.

Even with their support, I was full of cracks, and no amount of glue could keep me together. I still grieved for Shel, and now I had to grieve for my father too. It was a pain I would not have wished on my worst enemy. I was Eeyore, the *Winnie the Pooh* character, with a permanent rain cloud over my head. I never got to come out of the rain. It wiped me out and made me bitter. I cried at the drop of a hat, much to my embarrassment. I was only a fraction of myself.

I had taken some time off from school, but now I was back in my regular classes. It was a cruel joke that I had to get back into the swing of my life again. I had been an honor roll student, but now I struggled to concentrate, even though I gave everything my best. I was broken, but the world wanted me to pretend I was whole, and I was exhausted with it.

Losing a parent is an exquisite kind of agony that only those that have lost parents can understand. Dad had been with me since the beginning; he gave me life, sheltered me, dried my tears, cared when no one else did, laughed with me, cried when I cried, stood up for me, told me his stories, listened to my cares and worries, taught me everything I knew.

Suddenly, one half of the two people that had fashioned me was gone. It is a feeling of being utterly lost, and it is impossible to explain to someone that hasn't experienced it themselves. There would be no more birthday wish lists, no more Father's Day, no more long talks on the phone, no good-night hugs, no sparkling hazel eyes, no more of what made him my dad.

I was angry about some things, sad about others, and so incapable of handling it all. I wanted to cry to him about the fact that he was gone. I had gone to him for comfort for so many things in my life, but he wasn't there to comfort me over the loss of him. I still needed my dad. Thirty-one years was not enough. No one understood even if they did understand, and everything was patently unfair.

I couldn't properly grieve for Dad because I was still grieving for Shel. One day I would be in the middle of some mundane act, and suddenly the loss of my father would wash over me. I would cry hysterically in the most inappropriate place imaginable. I had premonitions about a grief that had not engulfed me yet. I tried to prepare myself for it, but I knew the reality would be worse than anything I could imagine.

I missed more work and school as I tried to pull myself together. A couple of weeks after Dad's death, I could function well enough to go back to my routine. I tried to go against the grain of my thoughts.

I'm not the only one that's been through a tragedy.

Life means that I will experience loss and I need to get used to it.

I am going to be okay. One step at a time.

I needed more time to heal. I tried to be patient with myself. I had to fake it until I could get everything under control. I returned to work and school and slowly started to get back into a rhythm.

Then the next sucker punch came.

CHAPTER 27:
GOING GENTLE INTO THAT GOOD NIGHT

*"H*ow are you holding up, Dee?" a nurse asked me, her eyes soft.

"I'm holding it together, but honestly, I cannot handle anymore loss. I really hope my family is spared from something horrible happening for a while," I responded as I hung my head.

"I hope that for you, too," she said quietly. She gave me a big hug before she walked away.

Two days later, on October 4, 2006, less than a week from the one-year anniversary of Shel's death, I got a phone call from my mother on my way to work. It was not even 7:00 a.m., and my windshield wipers worked hard to clear away the pouring rain.

She's probably calling to check on me, but it's awful early.

"Hi, Mom," I answered the phone.

"Hi, kid," she said, her tone flat. "I don't know how to tell you this, so I'm just going to get it over with. Grandma died this morning."

As soon as she said those words, I cried uncontrollably, as if the sorrow had been a bubble ready to burst at any moment.

"I know, honey," she said regretfully. "Are you at home?"

"No," I sobbed out. "I'm driving to work."

"Oh no! Oh, Dee, pull over. I didn't realize you were driving," Mom said worriedly.

"I'm turning around to go home, Mom," I cried as I took the next exit. "There is no way I can work today."

"Of course, you can't."

"How did it happen?" I worked to regain enough control to drive home.

"She died in her sleep last night."

"That's God being good to her," I said hoarsely. "She told me before that she wanted to go in her sleep."

Grandma had been God's faithful servant since she had accepted Him as her savior at the age of ten. A new wave of sadness washed over me as I realized how much Grandma meant to me. She had been my second mother, spiritual conscience, and confidante. She was another great love of my life gone.

A pause passed between Mom and me, and then I said, "I have got to go, Mom. It's raining and I need to pay attention."

"Okay, baby. Get home safe. I love you."

"Love you too, Mom," I said, and then hung up.

It was too much. There are no words for the depth of sorrow that struck me that day. My immediate regret was that I didn't call Grandma more during the three weeks since Dad's death. My mind had nagged at me to call her for the past two days. I had been busy trying to hold myself together. It was painful for me to talk to her.

We knew each other's sadness so well. I had talked to her a week before, and even though we had things to talk about, there were several pauses during our conversation. We seemed to get lost in our own thoughts. My hesitation to call her over the past two days came from the awkwardness of that phone call.

Give yourself a little more time before you call her again.

It made sense to me to avoid anything that caused me more pain, even if it meant that I avoided Grandma. Now we had run out of time.

I found comfort in the knowledge that she knew I loved her, but that missed phone call will always haunt me. I should have called, no matter how much it hurt. The regret of not doing so hurt me far more.

I was halfway home when I called my boss, Gwen.

"Hello?"

"Hi, Gwen. I'm sorry, but I won't be coming to work today. My grandmother has passed away," I said as my voice cracked.

"Dee! Are you serious?" she asked in astonishment.

"I'm afraid I am," I said softly. "I will need to go back to North Dakota again to attend her funeral."

"Oh, Dee, I'm so sorry. Yes, please take all the time you need. We'll see you when you get back."

"Thanks, Gwen, I appreciate it."

I disconnected the call and spent the rest of the ride home in one long sob. I was so shattered and scraped raw with emotion. Two days prior, I had stated that I couldn't handle anymore loss. It seemed to be a sick joke that I had to face yet another loved one's death.

I was adrift in some very rough seas, in fact drowning, with no boat or life preserver in sight. Another emotion plagued me, and it took me a bit to figure out that it was loneliness.

I slipped through her
And garnered strength
She showed me courage
Beyond any measure
I clung, I looked to her
And kindness was always shown

I was made to feel a treasure
She was the sun
And the moon and all in between
But put me before herself
A stronger woman I have never seen
And could never hope to be
But I pray fervently
A bit of her, a silken skein
Will entwine for all to see
And make me more of the person
She already believed me to be

—DW

CHAPTER 28:

GRANDMA

*I*f Grandma had to describe herself in one word, she would have undoubtedly said *Christian*. When I heard that she died, I lost more than a grandmother—I lost my spiritual compass. If I had a burning question about the Bible or God, or what I was doing on this Earth, I knew to go to Grandma with it. She would explain things to me in a way I could understand, and she knew which lessons would set me on the right path. Grandma would always ask me if I was going to church and if I prayed to Jesus. She was always curious about where I was on my spiritual journey.

Grandma knew I struggled sometimes, that I liked to put God on the back burner, but she never gave up on me. She prayed for me every day and hoped I would commit myself to the God she loved so much. I never gave her concrete evidence that I had done so, and I know she worried about me.

It was a habit of mine to send her poems, letters, and flowers for her birthdays and holidays, or simply because she was on my mind. She would ask my father in bewilderment, *What is that kid doing spending so much on me?*

It made me sad that there would be no more chances to show her I cared.

I spent so many nights with her and Grandpa as a child. We would get up on Sunday mornings and go to church together. Occasionally, we would stay home and do our own devotions. We would take turns reading the Bible, and she would explain what didn't make sense to me. We would tell stories and laugh. She was the type of grandma I could tell anything, and there would be no judgment. She would love me no matter what.

She would sit in a recliner with me curled up in her lap for hours and tell me stories about when she was a girl. I was captivated by her triumphs, lessons, disappointments, and miracles. Like my father, she was a great story-teller, and she kept me entertained until it was time to go home. I was always a little sad to leave Grandma's. I was safe, secure, and adored with her, and I didn't always feel that way at home. Her house became my escape. I never got tired of our visits, and I cherished our time together. It sustained me through a tough childhood, and I depended on her more than the average kid depends on a grandparent.

She was always there, ready to help, to give, and to believe in me. She made sure that I knew I was special to her. In a moment of reflection, I was horrified to realize that I had lost three of the most instrumental people in my life. Everyone I loved had families and busy lives of their own; but with these three people, the world stopped just for me. Shel, Dad, and Grandma had been the cornerstones of my life. I was defined by them, and I would never be as well-loved as I had been with them in my life.

The only cornerstone left was Brad. I loved him more than I thought was possible. But we weren't married, and he wasn't my family. He was my comfort, but he couldn't replace the ones I had lost. A powerful, profound sense of loss enveloped me, and I would never be the same. The woman that I was had died with them.

CHAPTER 29:
A BIG REGRET

*T*here are many things that I regretted after their deaths, but one regret in particular bothers me more than most. I missed Grandma's nineti-eth birthday. There hadn't been so many Wahls together in one place in many years. Pictures were taken, where everyone is all smiles, but I am not there. I look at my father in the pictures, and I see his impending death in them. I am convinced I could have helped him if I had been there. I look at Grandma's beautiful tiered cake, and her soft, sweet smile, and I hate myself for being the one to let her down. I let something as stupid as money get in the way.

You did the right thing at the time. Grandma understood that.

How could you have known what would happen?

Stop blaming yourself!

Dad and Brad both told me it was okay that I wasn't there, but it wasn't okay, and I knew it. It was more than an obligatory feeling. It was instinc-tual for me. Something told me to move heaven and earth to be there and I ignored it. I must live with that regret for the rest of my life. It was one of my last chances to be there, and show her I cared, and I failed her and myself. I should have sold something. I should have worked extra shifts. I should have done whatever I had to do, but I didn't, and there is nothing I can do about it now. All I can do is promise myself that it won't happen again with someone else that I love.

CHAPTER 30:
THE LETTERS

fter Shel died, I was bereft of the chance to tell him how I really felt about him. I comforted myself with the knowledge that he knew that I loved him, but I am not sure how much he heard in those last hours of his life. I'm not sure if he heard me say that he was the best brother I could have hoped for, or if he heard my last I love you.

I decided I would write letters to everyone I loved. Shel taught me that no day is a guarantee, and we need to tell people how we feel about them right now. I started by writing a letter to my grandma. Below is a snippet from the letter I had sent to her:

> *Thank you SO much for everything you have given me, Grandma. Thank you for loving me so much. Thank you for setting an example for me to follow. You are one of the greatest women I have known and will ever know. Your faith and strength are what I aspire to. God take care of you for me. Give yourself a big hug for me today and know I love you more than I could ever tell you.*

Grandma loved the letter. I was buoyed by her reaction and wrote one for my father as well. His was a little harder to write though. My feelings for him were complex. I didn't want the letter to be cruel, but I had difficult things that I wanted to tell him. Above all, I wanted the letter to be a celebration of our relationship. I wanted to let him know what he meant to me. The following is an excerpt from that letter:

The father that you are now is the one I'm going to remember above all. Right now, you are everything you taught us to be: strong, brave, intelligent, independent, and focused. You are a friend when I call you now, not just my father. You are pleasant to talk to and I no longer fear what will be on the other end of the line when I call. There is only you. I have always said . . . my dad would be the best dad in the world if he didn't drink. And you are, Dad. The best. Thank you for everything. Thank you for all the choices that led us to the family we are today and thank you for standing up for us and beside us during our journey. Our story isn't over yet, but I am looking forward to the ride from here!

Both Dad and Grandma received their letters a few months before their deaths. It gave me comfort to know they read my letters, but I was too spooked to write anymore. I had written two letters and there had been two deaths. Mom was next on my list, but I didn't have the heart to write one to her. I knew it wasn't rational, but I didn't want to risk it and tempt fate.

A different kind of letter came a few months after Shel's death. My father read it and promptly threw it in the garbage. Mom told me about it later, and I had to call and request a copy for myself. It was a letter from LifeSource to my parents. It detailed the outcome of the organs Shel had donated. Dad couldn't bear to read it, but I wanted to read that letter. It read as follows:

Dear Dee,

Please accept my heartfelt sympathy on the death of your brother, Shel. There are no words that can diminish the pain of your loss. But it can be a source of comfort knowing that other people may live better lives because of Shel's donation and your compassion for others.

On behalf of LifeSource, and those individuals waiting for transplants, I extend my deepest gratitude. Your brother's donation celebrates life: Shel's life and the lives of those he has given a second chance.

I hope the following information comforts you as you learn something about the individuals who benefitted from your son's donation. (Son is a typo of sorts, an obvious remnant from the letter they sent to my parents, which they modified for me.)

A 52-year-old man who suffered from hypertension received the gift of one of Shel's kidneys. This man has six children and is employed as a parts manager for a trucking company. He lives in Indiana and had been waiting for a kidney transplant since November 1996. This individual is fortunate to have received a transplant. Nationally, more than 63,000 people are currently waiting for kidney transplants. The medical staff said he is doing well since his transplant surgery. He is grateful for his transplant and wanted to say, "Thank you" to you, his donor family. Shel's donation and your generosity have given this man a chance for a longer and healthier life.

Shel's other kidney went to a 58-year-old man from North Carolina who had diabetes. He had been waiting for a kidney transplant since July 2004. This recipient has four children and twelve grandchildren. He works as a mechanic, provides tax preparation services, and enjoys fishing in his spare time. This man said he is "feeling great" since his transplant surgery, and he is looking forward to returning to work.

A 43-year-old man from Michigan received Shel's pancreas. This recipient is single and works as a farmer. He had diabetes and had waited for a pancreas transplant since June 2005. His transplant ended his need for insulin injections. Shel's gift and your compassion for others have given this man a future filled with hope.

Shel's liver went to a 32-year-old man who suffered from liver disease. He is married and has three children. He lives in Minnesota and previously worked in the computer field. This individual enjoys the game of soccer and spending time with his family. His name was added to the national transplant waiting list in September 2005. In this country, more than 17,000 people are currently waiting for liver transplants. He is doing well since his transplant surgery and said he "is thrilled". Shel has given this man and his family an extraordinary gift beyond measure.

For medical reasons, we were unable to transplant Shel's other organs. However, your willingness to donate is a gift in itself, offering hope to thousands of individuals waiting for life-saving transplants.

Again, thank you for helping us enable Shel to give the Gift of Life to others through his organ donation. Your brother is truly a hero. The grateful transplant recipients and their families will never forget his invaluable gifts.

There is an odd rush of emotion when you read an organ donation letter. I bawled as my loss rushed to the forefront of my brain again. I was angry that Shel had to die to help those people. At the same time, I experienced a bittersweet joy that Shel had helped those people. After reading the letter, I understood why Dad had thrown it away—it was very difficult to read. It was probably more so for Dad, as he had been the only one to object to Shel's organ donation.

As a young man, Dad knew his way around a Las Vegas mortuary that his friends owned. He knew too much and didn't want to put Shel's body through those procedures. It was only at the insistence of the rest of us that Dad finally agreed. As opposed as he was to it, Dad knew that Shel would want to help people live better lives.

I was grateful to have the letter. Occasionally, I still read it to remind myself that Shel lives on through those donations. His spirit is amplified through that act of selflessness. It was the obvious choice, given the way that Shel had lived his life.

Those three letters changed my life. The first two saved me from some regret. The last one was a bit of light shining through the darkness.

CHAPTER 31:
STOP THE LEAK

*B*rad did not feel comfortable taking more days off from work for Grandma's funeral. His employer had been nice about giving him time off for the other three funerals when we weren't married yet, but he didn't want to press his luck with a fourth one. I understood his feelings, but at the same time I wanted to beg him to come with me. It was going to be difficult to face everything alone. I steeled myself for the ride back to Bismarck. I was so tired in mind, body, and spirit. I wanted him to save me from everything. I wanted to fast forward to a time when I would be okay, if that was possible. I had doubts that I would make it through the turbulence that had become my life.

I called Brad as I headed out of town. I was the *Peanuts* character Linus, and Brad was the blanket I left behind. I was lost and terribly emotional as I drove further away from him. I called him for one last squeeze of the blanket, and he didn't disappoint me. We talked for quite a while, until I was well out of the twin cities.

"I'm not sure I can go back to that hospital," I told him. "I was burned out as a Health Unit Coordinator before this, let alone now. Every time I go back to work, it all comes rushing back to me."

"Well, that's up to you, Dee," he said quietly.

"I'm just not sure I can continue in the medical field. I lost the lottery for getting into nursing school and I don't feel passionate about it right now. I feel ready to wash my hands of it all. I don't think I can do it anymore."

"I understand, and it's your choice. I'm not sure if you're interested, but a position has opened where I work. It's entry-level, but it would get your foot in the door. I guarantee you'd get the job if you want it," Brad said.

"I'll think about it, thanks," I said absently. "I have to figure out where I want to go from here."

We talked for a while longer and then I let him go.

I had nothing to do but think on that road trip home. I listened to music and cried a lot. I would gather myself together and then break down all over again. It was a vicious cycle that repeated itself over the length of my trip. As my mind wandered, I was bombarded by memories of Grandma, Dad, and Shel. My car was a purgatory chamber.

My life was a mess. I didn't know how I would get through college. I didn't know how to go back to a job that had become a painful reminder of my loss. The radio kept me company but didn't assuage my pain. I wanted to hear a human voice, but I didn't want to bother Brad again. I decided to call Pastor Bob and Maggie.

Pastor and Maggie had been a source of strength for my faith ever since I met them at the age of fifteen. I could still see myself, a teenaged janitor at the small Nazarene church, my Walkman blasting music into my ears. I thought I was alone as I bopped around with the vacuum cleaner and sang out loud. I was startled by a kindly middle-aged man with a genteel smile.

Holy crap! How long has this guy been standing there?

He had popped out of nowhere, this strange man that smiled at me like we already knew each other.

"Hello! I'm Pastor Bob Annon, the new reverend of this church. How are you?"

"I'm fine, thanks," I mumbled. "I'm Dee Wahl. I clean the church."

"Well, it's a pleasure to meet you! I'll let you get back to it, but I wanted to say hello!"

I did not meet his wife Maggie until later. We were kindred souls and hit it off so well that we joked that we had known each other in another life. Our age difference did not hinder our relationship in the least. I would come to adore Pastor for his down-to-earth way of preaching, his easy smile, and affable manner. My family began to go to church because of them. Even Dad liked Pastor Bob—they had a mutual respect. Pastor Bob understood Dad and didn't judge him like other reverends had in the past. They became friends.

When I was nineteen and at a crossroads in my life, Pastor and Maggie announced that they had been *called* to another church. Dad called and asked them not to go, which shocked me. I realized what a loss it would be for my family, but mostly for me. I wanted to go with them to Sioux Falls, South Dakota. It is a testament to my dad's respect for Pastor that I was allowed to go. Eventually I grew restless and left them to move in with Tina in Fargo. Fast-forward a few years and they had settled in Carrington, North Dakota. I moved from Fargo to Bismarck, and then finally to the Twin Cities. They decided to retire in Carrington. They bought a house and renovated it into their dream retirement home.

I was way overdue for a visit to go see them. I picked up my cell phone and called them. I took a deep breath.

Get a grip. No crying!

I wanted to have a serious talk with Pastor Bob. I didn't want a crying jag to keep me from the questions I wanted to ask him.

"Hello! This is Pastor Bob," his voice boomed pleasantly in my ear.

"Pastor, it's Dee," I said. "Grandma passed away a couple of days ago. I feel so lost. I can't take anymore." I started to cry but the words continued to spill out. "I've lost Shel, Dad, and now Grandma. I can't stop my thoughts. I worry Dad is in hell. I can't find God in this, Pastor. Seriously, who loses four family members in one year? Tell me what to do, what to say, to get it to stop. I'm tormented by things I can't change, and I'm at the end of my rope. I want answers. Please help me."

"Pray for God to stop the leak," he said in the gentlest voice I'd ever heard him use.

"What?" I said in disbelief. "What do you mean, stop the leak?"

"Pray for God to stop the leak. If you pray with your whole heart and ask God for a miracle, He will stop the leak for you. The leak is the deaths, the pain, the torment, the insecurities, the sleeplessness, the shame, the regret, the guilt. Just pray to God for it to stop."

"It can't be that simple, Pastor," I said, as my teeth chattered.

"But it is. Honey, I believe your father made his peace with God before he passed from this Earth. Your grandma has gone home at last. And you are going to get through this and be okay. I promise you."

"I hope so," I said as I nursed my sniffles.

"Honey, I'm going to see you in a couple of days when we celebrate your grandma, and I'm gonna give you the biggest hug I've got," he said in his southern drawl.

"I look forward to it. I love you, Pastor. Thank you," I said softly.

"I love you too, honey. See you soon."

You're going to be okay.

His prediction sounded like something out of a dream. The weight I carried was a bit lighter after that call. I repeated his suggestion like a mantra, a heartfelt prayer I said out loud to the silence of my car.

Stop the leak, Lord. Please stop the leak. I can't take it anymore. Please . . . no more death for a while. I've had all I can bear, Lord. I'm begging you. Please stop the leak.

CHAPTER 32:
NEW SUIT FOR A SAD GIRL

I bought a new suit for Grandma's funeral. I got it from the Sears store in Bismarck's Gateway Mall. I was with my mother and Kathy. It was a black suit with thin purple pinstripes. I pretended it was for something other than a funeral.

I'll wear this out to dinner with Brad.

This will be nice for going to theaters in the cities.

I liked the idea that it was for something else. I didn't want to admit that this was a suit I would wear as I said goodbye to Grandma. I didn't want to think about it, so I made things up in my mind. I made a half-hearted attempt at cheerfulness.

Somewhere deep inside I had lost my mind, but I ignored the red lights going off in my head. To stay sane through this was such a bother. I was a hollowed-out, pitiful version of the girl I had been before, but it was a small comfort to pretend, so that's what I did.

I will paint the town red in this suit!

I pictured myself stronger. I would be a woman that laughed again.

I will go places and live life to the fullest!

I promised Shel I would live for him. It wasn't a lie—I would make plans. It was merely a truth I hadn't lived yet. I ignored a deeper, sinister voice that said I couldn't do it. I ignored the fear that I wouldn't make it out of the abyss.

CHAPTER 33:
I BOWED ON MY KNEES AND CRIED HOLY

*g*randma did not look like herself. Shel had looked wooden and vulnerable, Dad had looked younger and peaceful, and Grandma looked pinched and severe. Her bright hazel eyes and warm smile swept through my mind, and I hated to see her in that casket.

She was in that typical hand-on-top-of-hand casket pose. She wore a light blue suit, with a pink ruffled scarf around her neck. A little brooch was on her jacket lapel. In her hands, which gave me small comfort, she held a small white Bible, a handkerchief, and a silver cross. These personal touches were courtesy of Aunt Lettie. She was with her when they closed the casket.

I feel for morticians, I really do. They have a terrible task at hand. They prepare a person for their last viewing by everyone that has ever loved or cared for them. That must be extremely difficult, especially when they never knew them.

Grandma did not look like she did in life. Her cheeks looked pinned down and her mouth was in a grim line.

Maybe she died with a weird expression, and this was all they could do.

I didn't want that image of her to be my last memory of her; I knew that it would stick with me. It's a double-edged sword. To view her in the coffin helped me say goodbye, but it also harmed me, because that image burned into my brain. A scene from *Superman* popped into my head. He could go to a cave and see his dead parents, who were now holograms. There were pre-programmed answers to the questions that they knew he would ask in his lifetime. A part of me wanted that badly—a way to interact with them beyond the grave. Instead, I had these unwanted casket memories, some photographs, and a grainy videotape in a drawer somewhere.

Superman didn't know how good he had it.

Before the service began, I chatted with my brothers and their kids. We stood in a circle of comfort in the small church foyer. We eventually gravitated outside. It was early October, an unseasonably warm day, and the fall colors were beautiful in the sunlight.

I talked with Liz and her husband, Dave. Their son Isaac was playing with some other children. I was envious of their obliviousness of the situation. I wanted to forget for a bit and climb some trees.

We were at the Tuttle Nazarene Church for Grandma's funeral, and I had climbed many a tree there. I had walked into that church so many times with Grandma. Another wave of sadness engulfed me. How was I supposed to say goodbye to her? Maybe it should have been old hat for me by that point, but I wasn't any better at goodbyes.

We filed into the church, and I found Mom. I didn't have Brad this time, and she didn't have Dad, so we walked down the aisle together. I was the last one to enter the pew. To my left were Shannon, Shad, Carmen, Tammy, and the kids, along with various cousins and their families. I was supposed to be with them, not in the pew reserved for Grandma's children and their significant others.

I didn't care for rules at that moment. I clung to my mother, as the gravity of the occasion really started to hit me. Shel, Grandpa Jerry, Dad, and Grandma—they were all gone. I had sung my first hymn and slept on

Grandma's lap during sermons in that little church. All my sadness, terror, trauma, and emotion culminated all at once.

As I listened to my cousin Debbie read aloud a letter to Grandma from the pulpit, it happened; I had my first thoughts of suicide. It occurred to me that if I ended my life, I wouldn't have to live in this pain any longer. There was too much of it and I couldn't hold it all inside me. I wanted some relief, and death seemed like the answer.

Liz got up to sing, and it did not help me. Her hair was in ringlets of gold, her alabaster face beamed with love, and she sounded like an angel. I was so proud of her. She was so strong as she stood by that small altar, and her voice never faltered. I was jealous of her in that moment. Her final gifts to Grandma were these songs, and she sang them beautifully.

I sat in that pew and wanted to die. Deep in my bones, my body screamed that death was the answer, and I was embarrassed. I dissolved into tears, unable to hold anything back. I was slumped into the side of the pew, my composure completely gone. I could not stop the sobs that wracked my body. All my life, I had looked down on people that had committed suicide. They were weak, pitiful creatures. Now, here I was, at my greatest depth of despair and I got it. Finally, that emptiness, that desperation made sense to me.

Liz sang a song called "I Bowed on my Knees and Cried Holy." The lyrics clung to me, and I imagined Grandma in heaven. She met all her biblical heroes, and finally asked to see Jesus, the savior that delivered her from sin. It was exactly what Grandma wanted, but instead of finding that a comfort, I mourned the loss of her in my life.

The song made me hit rock bottom emotionally. I wanted to walk into Lake Josephine and never walk out again. I wanted to sink to the bottom of the lake that Shel had loved. After I drowned, the pain would be gone. The cold water would swirl around me and sting my skin as my lungs filled with water. I would deprive myself of breath and life. In my grief-addled brain, it made perfect sense. All I had to do was follow through with it.

Then something hit me like a lightning bolt. Comfort washed over me. Grandma was there, and everything she had been to me flashed through my mind in an instant. The answer was suddenly so clear. I wanted to be baptized. Once the thought took root in my brain, it spread like wildfire.

I will be baptized today! Please, Lord, let Grandma see it. Please help me do this today. I am ready, Lord Jesus.

I had toyed with the idea for years. It was something I wanted to do, but always found a reason to delay. Well, not today. I pushed aside my thoughts of suicide and embraced the savior I had known all my life. Jesus was my answer. For the first time in months, I had a tiny ray of hope. A small flame began to burn deep inside my soul.

I went to the reception at the Tuttle Senior Center. For many years, my grandfather had come here for his afternoon coffee. For a moment, I saw Harold and Lois Wahl playing bridge with their friends at the table in the corner. I shook myself from my reverie and made my way through the table of food set off to the side. I grabbed a cup of punch. My eyes scanned the room until I spied the faces I was looking for: Pastor Bob and Maggie.

I spent all my time there in conversation with them. Some people came to pay their respects to me, and I let them. I did not make any effort on my own. I had a single-mindedness about what I needed to do, and I didn't have much patience for anything else.

A man joined us at our table. I gave him a cursory glance and pursed my lips. He was no friend of my family.

Why are you here?

"How are you?" he asked with a Cheshire cat grin.

"I'm fine, considering my grandmother just died," I said dryly.

"Yes, so sorry for your loss," he said without a drop of emotion. "Well, what are you up to now?"

A creepy grin was pasted on his face. I couldn't help but give him a withered look.

"I'm in Minneapolis, working at Children's Hospital. I'm going to school to be a nurse." I pointedly went back to my conversation with Pastor Bob and Maggie.

"Well, that's great!" he enthused as he laughed out loud.

I gave a small smile and said nothing more.

He stared for a moment, but I didn't bite.

"Well, nice talking to you," he said with serious snark. He pushed away from the table in a hurry.

"You as well," I responded without a glance.

I am committing myself to my Lord today; everything else will need to wait.

"Would you mind doing a baptism today?" I asked Pastor with a smile.

"I would be delighted," he responded with a broad grin. "Did you want to go to Josephine to do it?"

I almost laughed. "No, I want to do it at Mom's house."

"Are you sure, Dee? The lake would be perfect."

"I get what you're saying, Pastor. But what could be more perfect than doing it at a house that knows the Wahl family so well?"

"Right you are," he relented, his eyes twinkling.

We made plans to go to the house shortly. I went on a search for Aunt Lettie.

I wondered briefly if it was selfish to become baptized on the day of Grandma's funeral. I did not want to detract from a reception in her honor.

She wouldn't want it any other way.

I had to do it that day. She was with me, and her smile filled my mind. Just as Shel had watched me from the treetops, it seemed that Grandma was all around me. Her happiness was almost tangible to me.

I wanted Aunt Lettie there with me. She was Dad and Grandma rolled into one, and I wanted her beside me.

"I would love to be there," she said in response to my request, her smile wide.

I didn't want a fuss made, but I mentioned it to a cousin or two, and soon nearly thirty people were going to witness my baptism. We all trooped up to Mom's house.

Pastor asked me to fill a pitcher of water. I was in the kitchen when I saw Shad. I'm not sure what prompted me to say it, but I said, "Would you like to be baptized with me?"

"As long as the water is pouring?" he asked with a hint of a smile.

"Yes, if you want to," I responded as I held his gaze.

"Yes, I do," he said to my great surprise. I smiled and filled another pitcher of water.

We stepped out into the front yard of the house. It was so beautiful. The yard was decked out in full fall splendor, the trees alive with vivid shades of red, gold, and orange. A slight wind caressed us, and the leaves swirled around the yard in a dance.

I stood in front of Pastor and met his gaze. He spoke about Shel, Dad, and Grandma, and said serenely, "I believe that all has been forgiven and that they have been reunited in heaven with our Lord Jesus Christ."

There was an almost audible sigh from those gathered. His compassionate voice and kind words were like a warm embrace.

"Dee, have you accepted Jesus Christ as your Lord and Savior?"

"Yes," I answered him, with my heart on my lips.

"Do you believe that Jesus is the Son of God, who died on the cross and on the third day he rose from the dead for the forgiveness of your sins?" he asked, his blue eyes unwavering.

With a joyful heart, I responded, "Yes, I do."

"Then in obedience to our Lord and Savior Jesus Christ, and upon your profession of faith, I baptize you, my sister, in the name of the Father, Son, and Holy Spirit," he said, and his clear, strong voice echoed triumphantly in my ears.

As he spoke, I bent my head. The cool water flowed onto the back of my neck. I had never been more alive in my life. It was the sweetest comfort I have ever known. That small flame that had flickered in the church spread through me like wildfire. There was immediate peace in my soul, as it was washed clean of my worry, fear, and grief. For the first time, I knew I was in the presence of Jesus. There was no doubt in my mind that it was Him there with me. I was saved, blessed, and comforted. I was whole. He gave me what no one else could at that time in my life—a reason to live.

It was strange, but I was fully there and yet outside of my body. I looked down and saw my feet, but I floated above myself. It was an incredible lightness of being that was not of this world. Colors were unnaturally bright but did not hurt my eyes. The warmth of the sun emanated from my core. I was in an embrace, but I was free and lighter than air. My sorrow, which had almost ended my life a few hours ago, was gone from me. I saw only beauty, light, and colors. There was only unspeakable joy and love. Everyone else fell away and I was completely in the moment with Him.

I moved my feet to make sure they responded to my brain, and they did. I wanted to scream for joy that this miracle was happening to me. I was fully myself. No stone unturned and no shame. I had heard of God, Jesus, and the Holy Spirit all my life, but they became real for me in that moment.

Some people turn from God, but I never blamed Him for what happened to me. I turned to Him in my weakness and confusion. That day, when all the deaths and sorrow culminated in that little church, I didn't think to come to Him. I looked for an easy way out. I was so low it didn't occur to me to do anything other than die. He pulled me out of the abyss when I couldn't go on any longer. He held me in the palm of His hand and showed me that I would heal. For that unconditional love, which only He can give, I am forever grateful. My baptism was an exquisite gift that came when I needed it most.

I watched as Shad was baptized. I smiled through my tears. I hoped he was feeling a fraction of the comfort and joy that coursed through me. I floated in an aura of peace and light. There was no pain, only an assurance that I would be okay. Something so remarkable had happened to me that I wanted to shout it from the rooftops. I blew my nose, cried a river, laughed with my whole heart, and hugged people that were so happy for me. Love was all around me, and it was incredible. I hugged Shad first, so hard and tight. We shared this unique bond, and it will always be ours to remember. I was bombarded with hugs from my mother and my brothers' families, my cousins, uncles, aunts, and friends. I knew that it was a very special moment in time, and I savored it as much as possible.

There are two things I remember the most: a comment from my cousin Brittany and a conversation with Maggie. As she hugged me, Brittany said, "You will always be beautiful to Him."

I smiled at her, but I didn't realize at that moment the gravity of her words. I have reflected on her words numerous times through the years. Times when I've been sad, when I've made mistakes and sinned. I didn't become this perfect person after that day. I swear when I'm angry, I make terrible decisions that hurt myself and others, and I say the wrong things to people. I sit in judgment of others when I have my own problems to address.

I'm not a saint; I'm a sinner who was reborn with God in my heart. That doesn't mean the road is always paved for me—it's much the opposite—but I remember that I am always beautiful to Him. There is forgiveness and I can move forward. I will always be a work in progress until the day I die and go to be with my Lord. I still don't call myself a Christian, because it seems too lofty of a title for me. All I know is that He is always there, even when I forget to ask, even when I make mistakes.

Maggie came over and gave me a bear hug, her face wreathed in a smile. "I'm so happy for you, honey. But I must ask you this: did you only get your neck wet?"

I knew exactly what she meant, and I smiled. "No, Mags, I didn't only get my neck wet. I'm committed to the Lord. I'm no good without Him, and I know it."

"That's good, because He died for you, girl."

"I know, Mags. I don't want to put Him on the back burner anymore. I'm serious about this. It's not just about my grief. I know He is real, and I won't turn my back on Him ever again. Don't worry about me. This is not a stunt. I want Him in my life always."

She hugged me again, for a long time, and then squeezed my shoulder as she walked away. I watched her go for a moment, and then was enveloped by more well-wishers.

We all visited for a while and then people started to leave. Sheila, my cousin Dave's wife, came over to me for a hug. She pulled back and looked me in the eyes, before she glanced at my mother. "Would you both like to come to our house tonight? Please come. Wear some really comfy clothes and we'll eat and chat."

Mom and I looked at each other, and no words passed between us. I smiled and said, "We would love to, Sheila."

Mom and I drove to Bismarck that night. We spent time with a side of the family that I didn't get to see very often. It was a blessing to sit around and reminisce with them. After a roller-coaster day, it was a sweet balm to hear their voices and see familiar faces. Dad had avoided these kinds of gatherings, and I was sorry for him. Booze, anger, and resentment had stolen so many relationships from him. Once again, I was aware of Grandma's smile in my heart. It was my hope that she had been with me through the events of the day. I knew she would be so proud of me, and I wanted it to be one more reason to dance in heaven. Out of the greatest of losses had come a victory. I hugged it to myself with all my might. I didn't have to pretend. I had it on good authority that I would be just fine. I needed only to believe in myself, and in my Lord and Savior.

A year of four seasons
A loss for every one
It took a year, my darling
For me to come undone
I wept with all my regret
My anger, sadness and fear
The losses were so many
During that fretful year
I faced the Lord with my pain
And He made it go away
For there never was a peace so sweet
As the day I called His name
He smiled as the water flowed
Pure again I became
He carried me through
As bittersweet memories remained
Never to be whole on this earth again
I'm doing the best I can do
For the Lord takes care of me, dear ones
Just as He takes care of you

—DW

CHAPTER 34:
LIFE CHANGES

I went back to the Twin Cities a few days later with renewed spirit. A euphoria that I can only describe as supernatural carried me in its tender care for weeks. I had answers to problems that had been plaguing me prior to my trip. For instance, I had Brad refer me for the job at Brocade. I interviewed for it and landed it within a week. I put in my notice at the hospital and finished out my two weeks with them. I also decided to change my major at college—I didn't want to be a nurse anymore. Sometimes bad things happen, and the focus and drive to accomplish career goals is intensified. It happened the opposite way for me. I no longer had the heart or passion to pursue the medical field. I had floundered before, but after I got back, I decided to end it. I could always choose it again.

Everything seemed so clear, and before I knew it, my life was completely different. I had new goals and ambitions. At times, I missed the rewards that line of work brought me, but not enough to go back to it. When I closed the door on that part of my life, it was with relief and little regret.

I decided to change my major to Business Administration. I already had many of the credits and I would have my degree in a couple of years. I headed back to school that fall. I worked twelve-hour shifts on weekends, so

I had plenty of time to complete my schoolwork. I fell into a steady routine and started to flourish at work and school. I finally owned my life again.

My euphoria wore off after a few weeks. I had good days and bad days. I really struggled at times, but I stayed with it and read my Bible regularly. If I had questions about the Bible, my beliefs, or God, I went to Aunt Lettie with them. I leaned on her heavily and wrote to her often. The more I read the Bible, the more I was comforted. The more I learned, the more I wanted to know. I was learning to have a real relationship with Jesus, and I came to Him with everything. I prayed to Him when I was sad, happy, discouraged, doubtful, or hurt. I held nothing back from Him. He already knew it all anyway. To have a real relationship with Him, He had to hear it from me.

When I was dark and nasty, I asked Him to help me conquer my fears. If something bad happened, I asked Him to forgive me and help me do better. If something wonderful happened, I praised Him and thanked Him for blessing me. I figured that coming to Him only when I was sad or hurt was half of a relationship. I wanted to share everything with Him. He was my Lord, Savior, best friend, brother, champion, father, confidant, and healer. I talked to Him daily—I still do. If Grandma were to ask me how I am, I'd say, "Don't worry about me, Grandma. I know the Lord and He knows me."

I am not a finished product. I constantly evolve and always try to do better. Jesus makes me want to do better. When I mess up, He tells me. It might be a voice in my head, a chide from my boyfriend, or the results of my actions. I glory in our relationship, and I pray that it grows stronger every day. He died for my sins, and it is by grace alone that I am saved. Once I got that, once I really opened my heart and soul to Him, life started to make sense. I am so thankful that I have realized the truth. I pray that everyone that reads this book finds that truth in their heart and is saved by it. Amen!

CHAPTER 35:
HORSES, MOTORCYCLES, AND YOGA

I cannot fully express how important it was for me to discover things that gave me a reason to live again. It was a slow, arduous process, but I learned to look for beauty where I could find it. My faith was a big part of my recovery, but I also realized I had to put in some of the work myself. I pushed past heartbreaking sadness, guilt, and depression and reached for life again when I was ready. I built myself up one small step at a time. Sadie was one step toward life. To enlist in school again was another. My therapy came in the form of my poetry and this book. Maybe I should have seen a therapist, but I decided that wasn't for me. Instead, and maybe more painstakingly, I devised my own therapy. I grasped at things that made me feel alive again.

I rediscovered my love of horses. I had adored horses as a girl. I saw a discount voucher for a horse stable only three miles from my home and I jumped at it. Initially, I wanted to ride like the wind, but it turned out to be for riding lessons. I found that I liked the structure of it. I learned how to ride English style, which was different from the casual Western style I knew from childhood.

English style was for people that competed. There were three plastic steps that helped me climb on to the horse. I was very tall and uncertain in the saddle. I wasn't used to my legs being tucked up under me like a jockey. I would bounce in the seat while the horse trotted. There was a certain way to hold the reins. I wasn't supposed to cross the reins, which was my instinct. I was to shorten the reins with my thumbs, which was odd. I had to sit up straight, yet somehow be relaxed in the saddle. My teacher was named Marlys and she barked orders at me from her perch in the center of the ring. I didn't mind because I wanted to learn. I appreciated her no-nonsense style.

I went every other Sunday. I worked hard at it and continued to improve. Marlys gave praise when praise was due. The first horse I rode was an older mare named Jazz. I fell in love with her. She was gentle but had plenty of spirit and took care of me. I stroked her velvety nose and led her back to her stall when we were done with our lesson. I brushed her down and readied her for her next rider.

There was something therapeutic about the lessons. A horse shows their soul through their eyes. I could see Jazz's intelligence, pride, and strength when I met her gaze. When I was ready to move on to my next horse, Mickey, it was like I had left a friend behind. I still visited Jazz after my lessons with Mickey.

Mickey was a different kind of horse. He was a jet-black gelding, well-muscled and a definite step up from Jazz.

"Not everyone likes to ride him," Marlys told me as I climbed into the saddle.

"We'll be just fine," I said as I tightened my grip on the reins.

Mickey was very willful and liked to do things his own way. I handled him with a firmer hand and didn't get intimidated by him. A couple of times, when he was particularly wily, Marlys fitted me with some spurs and a riding crop. I couldn't hide my grin.

I'm Annie Oakley now!

To me, an animal lover, it seemed barbaric to spur a horse and smack his haunches with a crop. Marlys assured me I was not hurting him. I realized she was right. Mickey didn't seem to mind one bit.

"He gets lazy if he's not reminded to pick up the pace," Marlys said with her trademark smirk.

I took lessons for several months and loved every moment of it. When I was in the saddle, the horse and I became one. There was something so spiritual about it. I enjoyed the bond of trust that occurs between rider and horse. I was almost giddy when I finished a lesson.

Unfortunately, the stable decided to cut me from their roster. Marlys explained that all casual riders were told the same news. They wanted to focus on school-aged children that wanted to compete. I was heartbroken at first. There were no other stables near me. Eventually I moved past those feelings and appreciated those nine months I'd had with Jazz and Mickey. I still miss it and keep my eye out for similar opportunities, but if none come, I'm thankful for the time I had at the stable.

I went from a real horse to a steel one. Several seeds had been planted along the way, and I decided I wanted my own motorcycle. I wanted the better view, the more comfortable seat, and the independence of it. I had never been a daredevil in my life—far from it—but this would be the daring, look-what-I-did thing that I accomplished as a woman in my thirties. Plus, I knew Shel would think it was cool. Deep down, I wanted to do it to please him.

The road to acquire my motorcycle license was far from paved. I was really scared of it at first. I wasn't sure I'd make it out of the parking lot. I also flunked my Motorcycle Safety Foundation (MSF) course the first time around. This course is a great way to get a motorcycle license. I was taught how to ride, was tested on an obstacle course, and should have gotten my voucher to take to the DMV for my motorcycle endorsement. It wasn't so easy for me. It took me two more attempts, but I finally got my motorcycle license. I enrolled in a college course and that made all the difference. My instructors truly cared, and I learned so much from them. When I held that endorsement in my hand, a delicious sense of triumph swept through me. I had finally slayed the dragon.

Pearl was my first motorcycle. She was a 1990 Harley Sportster 883, nicely upgraded, her cream-colored tank a custom job that I loved. She was a bit temperamental and showed her age a bit, but she was a great first motorcycle for me. I laid her down only once, when I hit some gravel and freaked out. I grabbed a handful of brake that sent her out from under me. Even with that scare, I was determined to learn how to ride her. I learned to love the ride, not the destination. I loved the smells, the sunshine, and the wind. I would look down, and when I saw the pavement rush past me, it was a thrill. I rode next to Brad with pure joy in my heart. I loved to tool around town on it or take the backroads. I truly appreciated how free I was on that bike. I could fly.

I loved that I was a woman rider most of all. But I wasn't your typical motorcycle woman. I was on the petite side, and I turned heads. The little girls were my favorite. They would ride in the backseat of their parent's car and wave at me with excited grins. I could practically hear them exclaim to their parents that a girl was on a bike. I would smile and wave back at them.

Eventually, I traded in Pearl for a beautiful jet-black 2009 Sportster 1200. I named her Raven. Raven was a huge step up from Pearl. She's a much smoother ride and she takes care of me when my inexperience shows through a bit. I can't imagine life without the ride. It's a heady, all-encompassing feeling to ride. After the loss of Shel, I needed that control. I took my life into my hands every time I rode, yet I was joyful instead of fearful. I was at one with nature, so close that I could touch it. Through rain, sunshine, cloudy, or windy days, it was an escape for me. I could ride myself out of the blues, out of a funk, out of my grief.

Motorcycling demands that you live in the present. When a rider is not fully engaged, using all five senses to the max, they could die. Some say it's a death wish to ride, but for me, it's a celebration of life. I had to exercise the utmost respect for my own fears and skills as a rider. The sky, the air, my breath—all were connected. I had to own it, give myself to it, and hope I lived to ride another day. Motorcycling was the gift that kept on giving.

Another way I found joy was through yoga. I have come to love yoga as more than exercise. It is another kind of escape for me. I find strength, joy, and perseverance on my mat. I am as fearless as I dare to be as I hold poses that I didn't know I had it in me to do. God is there when I'm on my mat. I have no other way to describe the peace that I find there. My favorite pose is called *dancer*. It is graceful and pure—a perfect balance of your body weight—and so beautiful when done right.

I especially adore hot yoga. The room is at a toasty one-hundred-and-three degrees, and it's as if toxins leave my body as I sweat through the poses. Everything that's not right in me is wrung out and I can start over again. It is perfect, tangible bliss and I try to hold on to that feeling for as long as possible. When it fades and I slip back into the muck, I practice again. I am always able to find what I need from my mat. I am so grateful to have found this new love in my life. Some of my fondest memories during that time in my life come from that tiny studio. I would step into the night, fresh from a sweat session, and drink in the cold, crisp air. The sky would be blanketed in stars. I would stop in the middle of the parking lot, close my eyes, and just breathe.

CHAPTER 36:
REMEMBRANCE

After I lost Shel, it was important to me to find ways to honor him. There were key dates that I would stop, take a breath, and remember. Shel's death anniversary, his birthday, and Christmas were big dates for me. For his death anniversary, I do something that celebrates life—I take a trip, a hike, or a motorcycle ride. I do something that reminds me that it's great to be alive. On his birthday, I do things that he loved to do. I eat Red Baron meat lover's pizza, play pool, or watch movies. I do things that keep his memory alive for me. I miss him the most at Christmas, so I make a snow angel every year for him. I decorate and play music for him. It's a time of reflection, certainly, but mostly it's a time of year to remember him and keep him close to my heart.

Something else I did for Christmas was request a ring with Shel's birthstone. Kathy got it for me, and I cherish it. When I wear the Shel ring, it's like I've taken him with me. Sometimes people comment on the ring and ask if it's my birthstone. I tell them the truth.

It is a remembrance ring for my brother. It is his birthstone, not mine.

I love it when his name rolls off my tongue again. I'm happiest when I do something that brings his memory back to life.

I listen to Sinatra when I miss Dad. When I miss Grandma, I read Bible verses that she loved. I will never forget them because I strive to keep them in my heart. I realize that to be a keeper of the flame is to open myself up to a bit of melancholy, but those memories become more sweet and less bitter as time goes by. For as long as I draw breath, they will be remembered.

The reality is that you will grieve forever. You will not 'get over' the loss of a loved one; you will learn to live with it. You will heal and you will rebuild yourself around the loss you have suffered. You will be whole again, but you will never be the same. Nor should you be the same, nor would you want to.

—*Elisabeth Kübler-Ross*

CHAPTER 37:
VICTORY IS MINE

I'm not going to tell you that I moved on and everything was wonderful. Time made things easier, but there is no fairy tale ending here. I had to learn to adapt to my new life. I learned how to lean on God, my boyfriend, my family, and eventually, my own strength. Life will never be the same, I know that. I had to rebuild myself one cell at a time, with a lot of help and a lot of faith. I still feel Shel, Dad, and Grandma with me, and I know they always will be. I take comfort in all they meant to me and that will never change. For me, it is as if they are in the next room.

Tears gradually gave way to laughter when I thought about them. My memories became a source of strength and comfort, instead of pain. I came to realize that they were each in my life for a reason and that I was blessed to have them in my life at all. Shel was my great teacher and one of the few people that always loved me unconditionally. Dad was also a teacher of mine and taught me many lessons, the greatest of which was how to forgive. Grandma was a shining, spiritual example for me, and I still lean on her wisdom to this day. They were each a gift to me. I'm thankful they touched my life, even if our time together was far too short.

I will never be the same person I was, but I am the sum of all these experiences. They have made me the woman I am now. That woman is strong, capable, full of spirit, and ready to begin again. I haven't cured cancer, eliminated traffic for all, or done anything that grand, but I did survive my own life crises. I am a better person for it. It's made me more empathetic, kind, and caring. I'm a bit of an introvert, so it takes a bit of effort, but I try not to be so guarded anymore. I give people comfort when I see they need it. I don't resist the urge to be a light when I see darkness in others.

I seek out my Lord and Savior when I need Him. I realize that each day I have on Earth is a gift. It sounds funny, but I had to teach myself how to be happy. For a time, especially when I thought of Shel, I didn't think I deserved to be happy. I wondered why God took him and not me, when he had so much life left to live.

Then I realized that I shouldn't second-guess God. He has His reasons for everything that happens to me. All the pain, suffering, and loss, it's not for nothing. And think about it, is there anything we go through that Jesus did not go through Himself during His life on Earth? We are here to learn. We are here to be tested. Whatever happens on my journey, I believe it is for the betterment of me. God is in control, but so are we. There are choices we make every day, good and bad, and He waits for us to come to Him with all of it.

When I lost Shel, Dad, and Grandma, I believe He cried with me. He carried me. He loved me. I don't know why they had to die, and it's not my job to know. That's for God to know, and for me to know someday. There are answers I won't know in this life, but I will in the next. He has all the answers, and that is a comfort to me. I can lay my troubles, fears, and sorrows at His feet.

Lord, I can't bear this anymore, please take this from me.

He waits, so patiently, for us to break down, to lean on Him, to realize we need Him.

Lord, I keep taking on things I can't handle. I must give them back to you. Thank you for your patience with me.

When I learned to let go and put my trust in Him, things got easier for me. Don't get me wrong, it's not like I was cured of a disease. I still had my troubles. I still had pain. I had to climb a huge mountain of grief, but it was much easier with Him as my partner. He gave me the strength to take back my life and do something with it.

And then there is Brad. God is my heavenly rock, and Brad is my earthly one. I was no longer the woman he fell in love with, but he took me for better or worse, before any vows were spoken between us. We can look at each other from across a room and hold conversations without a word spoken. There is a shorthand between us, a connection, that sustained me through the worst time of my life. Others might have run for the hills, but Brad stayed beside me through it all. He will always be my safe harbor.

I am a woman who has figuratively climbed Mount Everest. I am a survivor. I have my faith. I find beauty in every day. I have loved and lost. I still love. I will always love.